LEARNING TO
RIDE

LEARNING TO
RIDE

SHEILA ROUGHTON

BHSI

WARD LOCK RIDING SCHOOL

WARD LOCK

A WARD LOCK BOOK

First published in paperback in the UK 1995
by Ward Lock
Wellington House
125 Strand
LONDON
WC2R 0BB

A Cassell Imprint

Distributed in the United States
by Sterling Publishing Co., Inc.
387 Park Avenue South, New York, NY 10016-8810

Distributed in Australia
by Capricorn Link (Australia) Pty Ltd
2/13 Carrington Road, Castle Hill NSW 2154

A British Library Cataloguing in Publication Data block for this book may be obtained
from the British Library

ISBN 0 7063 7422 3
Typeset by August Filmsetting, Haydock, St Helens
Printed and bound in Great Britain by Hillman Printers (Frome) Ltd

Frontispiece: Riding in the open can be an exhilarating experience.

CONTENTS

THE AUTHOR

SHEILA ROUGHTON has many years' experience of training both horses and riders. She has competed at International level and is a BHS Chief Examiner and currently a full time lecturer at Moulton College, Northampton. She has recently turned her hand to writing and from first hand experience has produced several practical books, aimed at riders of all levels.

ACKNOWLEDGEMENTS

My thanks go to my father Geoffrey Chandler for the hours of helpful advice and encouragement, Mary Cheney for deciphering my writing and typing the manuscript and Thorney Equestrian Services for the photographs. Without their enthusiasm throughout, the task would have seemed endless!

I would also like to thank Rachel Rowlatt, Lisa Lemon, Emma Roughton and Derek Payne for demonstrating my ideas and Moulton College for the use of their facilities.

INTRODUCTION

Before you start learning to ride, it is important to know a little about the handling of the horse. Horses are not humans, and one of the greatest barriers to the understanding of any animal is to give it a human personality. You must learn about the natural instincts of the horse so that you can develop a sympathetic understanding of its needs and reactions.

Horses by nature are very nervous creatures and they need quiet, confident handling. The horse has two ways of telling you how it is feeling: by the position of its ears and the expression in its eyes. A horse that is nervous or frightened will probably have its head up, its eyes will be staring, its nostrils distended, its ears over-pricked and the muscles on its neck will be tight. A bad-tempered horse will have its

A quiet, happy horse.

ears flat back and will show the white of its eye.

A relaxed, happy horse will stand relaxed and look up as it hears you approach. It will either ignore you and continue eating or prick up its ears and give you a welcoming whinny.

APPROACH

When approaching the horse in either the field or the stable, always speak quietly in greeting. Have your left hand extended, with the palm of your hand uppermost and the fingers straight. Pat and stroke the horse's neck and near shoulder (the horse's left shoulder) with your right hand without startling it. Normally your approach should be from the near, or left, side. Should it be necessary in certain

A bad-tempered horse with its ears back and mouth open.

circumstances to approach from the off, or right, side, the action of left and right hand will be reversed. If approaching the horse in a field from the conventional side, place the headcollar or halter over the horse's nose with the left hand and fit the headpiece over the horse's poll with the right hand.

When handling the horse, always reassure it quietly by talking to it and by progressively touching it towards the point at which you want to arrive. For example, when picking up a foreleg, first touch the horse on the shoulder, sliding your hand down the forearm, past the knee and down the tendons to the fetlock. Gently lean with your shoulder against the horse's shoulder to put its weight onto its opposite leg. Firmly grasp the fetlock with your inside hand and ask the horse to lift its leg by saying 'up' and squeezing the joint.

When dealing with the hind leg the procedure is similar to that with the front leg. First place your hand on top of the horse's quarters, slide it down the leg to the hock, and then move your hand round to the front of the leg and run it down until you reach the fetlock, when the leg can be raised. Never leave your arm behind the horse's leg in case it kicks, as this will result in your arm being broken. If the horse is known to be liable to kick, you can grasp its tail with your outside hand and hold it across the leg about to be lifted. Should a kick be imminent the tail dock will stiffen, indicating that problems are about to arise.

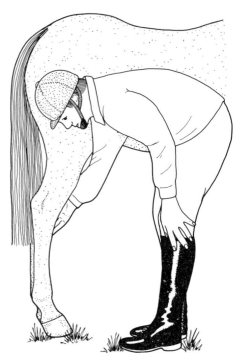

Picking up the near hind foot, being careful never to leave your arm behind the horse's leg.

When dealing with the horse's lower leg or foot never kneel, always crouch. Should the horse for any reason become startled and move quickly to the side, the crouch position will allow you to get out of harm's way.

Whenever possible, walk round in front of the horse. If you find it necessary to pass round the rear of the horse, you must alert it to what you are doing. This can be done either by placing a hand on its quarters as you pass by, or by holding onto the tail. In either case, pass close to the horse. This, should the horse kick, will result in a push rather than a metal-shod punch.

CHAPTER 1

THE BASICS

Top competitive riders manage to make riding a horse look quite easy. However years of work, dedication, practice and experience go into the production of the apparently easy skills that they demonstrate. Do not, however, be put off by this. Remember that they, too, had to start somewhere, and have had their share of disappointments and moments of frustration.

The best way to learn is to patronize a good riding school that employs qualified and experienced teachers. There you will receive a reliable assessment of your capabilities and be provided with a suitable mount on which to learn the basics. Having learnt these safely and enjoyably, you will be able to continue gaining experience by practising at home on your own horse, with regular visits to a professional instructor for assessment of your progress and advice on future work.

The horse does not have great intelligence, a fact that enables it to be ridden in the first place, since it is physically much stronger than humans are. The horse does, however, have an extremely long memory and you must remember this, especially when dealing with a young horse. A moment of anger, frustration or unjustified

punishment could cost many hours of work in the future to re-establish its confidence.

CLOTHING FOR THE RIDER

Whether you are attending a riding school or practising in your own paddock, it is essential to consider your clothing and equipment. Safety is of paramount importance, and comfort or the lack of it may affect your performance.

An absolute must is a properly designed, well-fitting hard hat with a chin-strap. There are two main types – the velvet cap based on the traditional hunting cap, and the crash helmet similar to those worn by National Hunt jockeys. The velvet cap has a flexible peak and a chin-strap secured to the cap at three points.

It is advisable to wear a back protector, which will prevent you bruising your back and ribs in the case of a fall. The newest ones come in a vest design and provide protection not only for the back but also for the kidneys, ribs, shoulders and the front of the body.

If you are wearing a jacket, it must be properly buttoned up. A flapping jacket not only looks

slovenly, it may distract or frighten the horse. It should fit well, especially across the shoulders. Too tight a jacket prevents correct movement of the upper arm, too large a jacket gets in the way of rein control. Either will be uncomfortable and distracting. Remove any jewellery before mounting. Earrings and necklaces can get caught and cause nasty tearing or burns. Rings on fingers can also get caught, which could, at the worst, amputate a finger.

Although jeans are often worn by riders, they are not really suitable for the serious rider. They are loose at the knee and wrinkle, causing soreness and a less secure contact with the saddle. They also tend to ride up the leg, depriving the rider of protection from the stirrup leathers. It is best to wear a pair of tight-fitting jodhpurs designed for the job.

Footwear is almost as vital as a hard hat for safety. Best is a proper riding boot, or jodhpur boot. If the latter, choose the elastic-sided variety, not those that strap around the ankle as the buckle has been known to become caught in the stirrup iron and in any case restricts the suppleness of the joint. A pair of stout walking shoes with a medium heel is the next-best choice, but the same precaution must be taken – no buckles, fancy tongues or ornamentation to trap the foot in the stirrup. Completely out are heel-less trainers, slip-ons and sandals, as

these are liable to slip through the irons and may lead to a serious accident. High-heeled fashion boots may also become trapped.

Although it is advisable to employ the services of a qualified, experienced instructor, there will be times, if you own a horse, when you will wish to practise at home. Always have an assistant with you when you are jumping. If that assistant is also knowledgeable, so much the better because then you will have a 'talking mirror' to tell you exactly what you or your horse is doing, something one cannot always tell from the saddle. Even if the assistant knows nothing about equitation, he or she will be available to help, or run for assistance should an accident occur, and will be invaluable picking up poles or altering fences, or even catching a loose horse.

EQUIPMENT FOR THE HORSE

The best bridle for a horse being ridden by a novice is either a rubber or a plain-jointed snaffle, preferably with a thick mouthpiece to the bit and egg-butts. This type of bit will protect the horse from the worst effects of any involuntary movements, caused by loss of balance, from the beginner's hands, which tend to be somewhat insensitive in the early stages. Should the horse require a stronger

It is essential that you wear a hat that complies with legal safety standards and suitable footwear with a medium-sized heel. Jackets must always be done up.

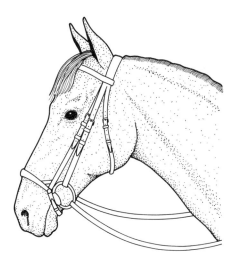

A correctly fitted egg-butt snaffle bridle with a drop noseband.

type of bit, it is probably the wrong horse for use as a learner's mount.

Saddles come in one of three main designs – dressage, jumping or general-purpose. For the serious competitor or specialist rider, more than one saddle becomes necessary. You cannot expect to be comfortable, or successful, using a dressage saddle for jumping, and without the deep seat and balanced central position afforded by the dressage saddle ultimate control of the horse in this discipline would be lost. However, as far as the novice rider, the non-specialist rider or the merely impecunious rider is concerned, there is the alternative of the general-purpose saddle. It is not as good as a dressage saddle for dressage, or a jumping saddle for jumping. However, for the novice and the non-specialist rider, the general-purpose saddle is perfectly adequate, and a good one will last for very many years.

The general-purpose saddle will have a reasonably deep seat and a spring tree. It will have well-padded knee-rolls on the saddle flaps. The object of the saddle is to provide the rider with maximum security, control and comfort and to assist in the correct positioning of the rider. To fulfil all of these requirements the saddle must be the right size for the rider as well as for the horse. The position of the knee-roll is also important. If it is too far forward for the rider's knee, it will serve no useful purpose. If it is too short, it will not only interfere with a correct position, but will cause very painful sores on the inside of the knee.

Equally, of course, an ill-fitting saddle will cause the horse pain and, if its use is persisted with, lasting damage. It is essential that the saddle fits the horse. Briefly, the following points require attention.

The weight of the saddle should be evenly distributed from front to rear over the muscles that cover the upper part of the ribs, on which the rider sits. There should be no weight on the loins.

There must be no pressure on the horse's spine. Places where this may occur are at the back of the saddle, especially when the saddle is on the small side for the rider, or in the centre of the channel at the time when the horse rounds its back over a jump. The latter happens most frequently with the deeper-seated saddle and its effect is minimized by the use of a numnah. This is not to suggest that a numnah is a device to make ill-fitting saddles fit. It should not be used for that purpose, because it cannot do it satisfactorily.

A properly fitted general-purpose saddle with a reasonably deep seat and padded knee-rolls.

It protects the horse and is more comfortable when it is using its back energetically.

The withers should not be pinched (i.e., front arch too narrow), nor pressed upon (i.e., front arch too wide or too low).

The play of the shoulder blades must not be hampered.

While on the subject of saddles, a word about girths is appropriate. Whatever type of girth you use, never rely on just one buckle. Most types of leather girth, the string girth, the nylon girth and the cottage craft girth, all have two buckles. These should be attached to the first and second girth tabs or the first and third, *never* the second and third. This is because the front girth tab is attached to the saddle by one piece of webbing and the second and third tabs share another piece of webbing. It is very unlikely that both pieces of webbing will go at the same time, so should one give way the saddle will still stay in position. Some saddles, however, only have two tabs. Check whether these are attached independently. If they are there is no problem. If they are not, you should not use that saddle. The stirrup irons should be made of stainless steel and have rubber treads fitted to the base to prevent the feet from slipping right into the iron, i.e., the foot being 'home' in the iron.

Another useful piece of equipment for both horse and rider is a neck-strap. It will help a rider maintain balance over undulating country or when jumping, especially over trappy natural obstacles. Many a running martingale has been fitted to a horse, not because the horse needed it but to provide anchorage for the rider! The benefit to the horse, of course, comes from the fact that the rider no longer depends on the reins to balance, so gives the horse fewer jabs in the mouth. Neck-straps can be very simple, such as a spare stirrup leather, or a more elaborate hunter breastplate.

All saddlery must be cleaned regularly not only to preserve the leather and promote suppleness, but also to check it for signs of wear or damage. Particular attention should be paid to the stitching at the buckle end of the stirrup leathers, stitching on girths and reins. If wear is detected, the item should be discarded until repairs are effected.

The safety catch on the stirrup bar should always be open when riding. It is only closed when the horse is being led or when the saddle is being carried on the arm.

CHAPTER 2

MOUNTING

There are four normal ways of mounting a horse, but before any of them are attempted, you must make sure the equipment is safe and fits the horse. As described in Chapter 1, the horse should be fitted with a snaffle bridle. The bit should fit comfortably in the horse's mouth, and there should be ample room for the ears, browband and throatlash. Always check the tightness of the girth just before mounting, because many horses will 'blow themselves out' when the saddle is first put on. This means that as the saddle area warms up the horse will relax and the girth become slack. The girth must be secure enough to prevent the saddle slipping over to one side as you put your foot in the stirrup. Also check that the flaps of the saddle are lying flat, and that the buckle guards are pulled down on both the near and off sides to cover the buckles of the girth. This is to prevent the girth buckles damaging the saddle flap. You can adjust the stirrups to approximately the correct length before mounting by standing to face the saddle and putting the knuckles of your right hand against the stirrup bar of the saddle. Hold the stirrup leather along the underneath of the arm so that the stirrup iron reaches into your armpit.

Mounting is generally done from the horse's near side (the left-hand side) although it is useful to be able to mount from either side. Stand with your left shoulder to the horse's near side, your shoulder facing its tail. Then, if the horse moves forward while you are mounting, the movement will help to lift you. If you face the horse's front end, and it moves forwards, you would be pulled forwards and downwards thus injuring yourself and/or frightening the horse. Having faced the tail, place your left hand on top of the neck, just in front of the withers. With the right hand turn the rear of the stirrup iron clockwise so that the stirrup leather will be lying correctly against the leg when mounted. It is very important that the horse stands still while being mounted, and should be held by an assistant while you are learning to mount. Have both the reins in your left hand, short enough to prevent the horse from moving.

Put your left foot in the stirrup and push your toe down so that it does not dig the horse in the ribs. This takes a lot of practice and a supple ankle. Pivot around on the right leg to face the horse and put the right hand on the far-side saddle flap, the pommel or the near-side saddle flap rather than twist the saddle tree by holding on to the cantle. Your left hand rests on top of the neck or withers and helps you to get up from the ground. Spring up from the left leg and lift the right leg over the top of the hindquarters, and lower yourself lightly and quietly into the saddle. If your leg touches the hindquarters as it swings over, it may frighten the horse and throw you off balance.

Once you are sitting quietly in the saddle, put your right foot into the stirrup by turning the front of the iron clockwise and placing the ball of the foot onto the tread. While the reins are in one hand, check the girth again before moving off. Take up the reins in both hands. The way to sit and hold the reins is explained in Chapter 3. If you are carrying a stick while mounting hold it in your left hand so that it can remain still and does not frighten the horse, or poke a willing helper.

When you have mastered the art of mounting, try mounting from the other side. Mounting from the off side (the right-hand side of the horse), the method is reversed and the right foot is put into the stirrup.

MOUNTING FROM A BLOCK

This method is highly recommended nowadays as everyone becomes more aware of the damage that can be done to horses' backs when they are mounted from the ground. Horses were designed to wander from place to place grazing continually, and to run away from danger. Their backs were not designed to carry humans, and certainly not to be twisted and pulled as more unathletic riders struggle to heave themselves into the saddle! A mounting block can be anything that provides a small secure platform approximately 60 cm (2 ft) high. A specially-designed block will have one or two steps on which the rider stands when mounting the horse. The method is to get the horse to stand with its near side parallel and close to the platform and continue mounting as described previously when mounting from the ground. Away from the stable yard a gate, a milk crate or similar article can facilitate mounting.

LEG-UP

For this method of mounting you will need an assistant. The rider faces the horse and carries out the mounting procedure as before except that the person giving the leg up provides the extra 'spring'.

Lift the lower part of your left leg behind you, bending it sharply at the knee. Your assistant should stand to the left and a little behind you and hold your left leg by putting their left hand under your knee and their right hand under and just in front of your ankle. As you give or duck to spring (it can be done on the count of three), the assistant should lift your leg firmly, taking most of the weight on your knee. When you are high enough, you can put the right leg over the hindquarters and lower yourself gently into the saddle. At this point your assistant releases the left leg and you continue as for conventional mounting. The extra 'spring' given to the rider is essential in order to achieve a neat and effective leg-up. If you are wearing highly polished leather boots for the leg-up, any marks made on the polish during the process must be removed with a duster once you have settled in the saddle.

riders keen on vaulting, and requires considerable agility. The spring must carry the body right on top of the withers and be powerful enough to allow you to straighten your arms. The procedure is then the same as for conventional mounting – you lift the right leg over the quarters, and so on. It is useful on many occasions, especially when you are in a great hurry, as it can be performed while the horse is moving forward.

VAULTING-UP

Vaulting-up from the ground is the invariable practice of racing lads or

DISMOUNTING

To dismount, put the reins and stick

The leg-up, showing the position of the assistant. It is essential for the rider to spring into the saddle without touching the horse's hindquarters.

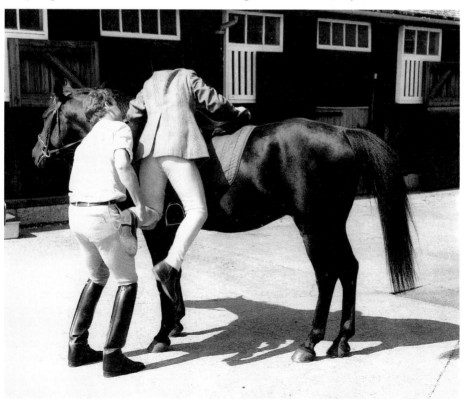

into the left hand and put both hands on the horse's neck. Remove both feet from the stirrups, lean forward, and swing the right leg back and over the horse's hindquarters, taking care not to touch them. Vault lightly to the ground, bending the knees as you land. Then turn to face the horse's head, keeping hold of the reins. If finishing a ride, run up the stirrups on each side, loosen the girth and take the reins over the horse's head ready to lead it back to its stable.

Remember

1. Check all equipment for safety and comfort before mounting.
2. Adjust the stirrups to approximately the correct length.
3. 'Spring' and agility are required from the rider for all forms of mounting to prevent damage or discomfort to the horse.
4. The right leg must clear the quarters both mounting and dismounting.
5. The rider's weight must always be transferred gently into the saddle.
6. Never step down from the horse using the stirrup.

CHAPTER 3

THE BASIC FLATWORK POSITION

If you are in the correct position from the beginning, you should feel more comfortable and secure, and enjoy it more. You will also be able to apply the aids correctly and therefore communicate with the horse more easily. The instructor in turn will be able to work in safe, progressive steps so that you and the horse achieve your ambitions safely and with the least trouble.

In the correct position you will be able to sit comfortably, remain in balance with the horse, and apply the aids correctly. The horse's centre of balance is just behind the withers when it is standing in halt and when it moves at a slow pace. As it moves faster or jumps the balance moves forward. You must try to match the point of balance. At high speeds, such as gallop, or when jumping, the rider's weight must be further forward. Conversely, at slow and more precise paces, such as those used in dressage, the rider can apply the necessary aids from a more central position. This explains the

difference between the crouched position adopted by the steeple-chase rider as opposed to the upright, Grand Prix dressage rider.

THE SEAT

The foundation of a good and effective position is the seat. You should sit in the central, deepest part of the saddle. Your seat bones should take equal weight, with the spine pointing directly to the horse's spine. The muscles in the seat must be relaxed so that you can sit as deep as possible in the saddle. The two seat bones form two points of a triangle at the back, and the crotch or fork at the front of the seat makes the third point on which to base the position. When you are sitting correctly, your weight will be in the middle of the triangle. When the weight is kept in the centre of these points the pelvis will automatically be at the correct angle. An easy guide is to keep the seam of your breeches vertical to

Sitting in the correct position will enable you to sit comfortably, remain in balance and apply the aids correctly.

the ground. What are generally referred to as the hip bones are in fact the top of the pelvic girdle. These must be vertical to the saddle.

If you put too much weight on the seat bones and sit with your seat tucked under, the pelvis will get behind the vertical line. The back then becomes rounded and the leg slides forward. If the pelvic bones get in front of that vertical line, you are said to be 'sitting on the fork'. This encourages you to lean forward and the lower leg slips back. If either of the above faults occur, they will throw you out of balance

and therefore create stiffness in your efforts to stay on. They will also reduce the effective use of the seat later on. Any correction that you make to the leg position without altering the seat will cause your leg muscles to stiffen, producing a 'clothes peg' effect that pushes you up out of the saddle.

THE LEGS

The top of the legs in a human being are naturally in an upside-down V shape, so to accommodate the width of the horse this needs to become an upside-down U shape. To allow this to happen, the muscles in the seat and those of the thigh must be totally relaxed. The legs must lie as close as possible around the horse's sides with the thigh flat against the saddle and turned inwards from the hip. Men usually have flatter thighs than women, and any spare thigh muscle must be pulled to the back of the thigh. The knee must lie comfortably against the saddle without tension. This will allow the lower legs to hang down around the horse's sides, with the feet parallel to the horse's sides. The ball of the foot rests on the stirrup iron and a supple ankle joint will allow you to sink your weight down through the heel. This gives you the whole length of your foot on which to balance instead of just the 5 cm (2 in) provided by the stirrup iron.

The heel should be the lowest part of the foot, but some people find it difficult, if not impossible, to lower the heel without experiencing extreme stiffness in the ankle joint. Of the two evils – a slightly high heel or a stiff ankle joint – the latter is worse, but this does not excuse you from trying. Some people's conformation makes it easier or more difficult to attain the correct position of the leg in that the natural direction of the foot may be to the front or turned out. In attempting to correct this, it must be stressed that the whole leg must be turned inwards from the hip, as a correction of the foot alone will lead to a stiff ankle joint and weight being taken on the outside of the ball of the foot.

Common faults

1. Stiffness.
2. The legs pivot forwards, putting the rider behind the movement of the horse.
3. The legs pivot backwards, tipping the rider onto the fork.
4. The back collapses and the rider becomes round shouldered.
5. The arms stiffen and the hands are held low.

THE BACK

The back must be upright, with the spine erect and centred directly above the spine of the horse. It must be supple and relaxed so that the horse's movement can be absorbed by the hips and the small of the back. It takes several years of 'correction and relaxation' to train the human body to be able to cope with the altering movements of the horse. The shoulders must be square but without stiffness, with the head directly on top of the spine. You must look straight ahead between the horse's ears. The head is a heavy part of the body, and if you get into the habit of looking down it will encourage you to lean forward and round your back, becoming ineffective and out of balance.

You should try to be aware of your deportment at all times during the day – when walking, driving, sitting, and so on – to make it easier to sit on a horse correctly. Good deportment will help you to achieve a good position more easily. When

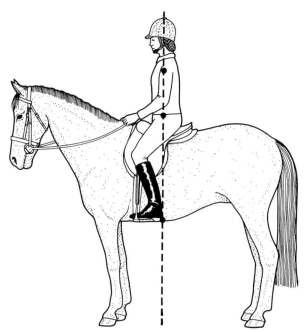

The basic flatwork position with an imaginary line drawn down from the rider's ear to the point of shoulder, through the hip to the heel.

you are sitting on a horse, it should be possible to draw an imaginary vertical line from the ear to the point of the shoulder, through the hip to the heel. This position is maintained at halt, walk, sitting trot and canter. In the rising trot you should incline the body slightly forward from the hip.

THE ARMS AND HANDS

The upper arms must hang naturally down beside the body with the elbows bent and the forearms inclined slightly inwards. Your hands join the arm to the reins and are held in front of the body with the thumbs uppermost, your right forearm pointing in the direction of the horse's left ear, and vice versa. Looked at from the side, there

should be a horizontal line from the bit, along the rein, through the little finger to the elbow. There should be no bend in the wrist when viewed from the side or from above. The arms must have no tension in any of the joints so that the feel you give the horse is sympathetic. You should think of the hand, wrist and forearm as an extension of the reins so that in effect you are riding from the elbow.

When you take up the reins, the weight you feel in the hand is what is known as the contact. This contact must not be too light or too heavy, but give a confident feel to the horse. With the arm in the correct position the hand and wrist will allow an 'elastic' connection with the reins, enabling the horse to go forward without pain or discomfort.

22

HOLDING THE REINS

The rein in your hand comes directly from the bit and passes between the little finger and the third finger. It then passes up across the palm and out of the top of the hand, over the index finger –

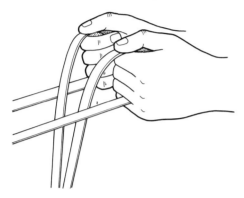

Holding the reins correctly.

secured by the thumb. The spare loop of rein should hang down the side of the withers.

The length of the rein is important because if it is too long, your body will lean back behind the vertical with the elbows out. If it is too short, it will encourage you to lean forward. If the back of your

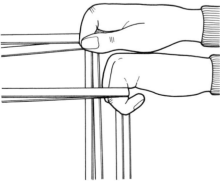

Flat hands.

hand turns uppermost the hand is then said to be flat. Flat hands are hard and give the horse a very unsympathetic feeling. Both hands must be held at equal height above the horse's neck.

Throughout training every rider is learning to sit comfortably and securely while producing the best effect on the horse by being able to communicate effectively. Your aim is to develop a seat independent of the reins to maintain balance, and to transmit clear and accurate signals to the horse. To relax all your muscles and still retain an upright, straight posture takes years of practice. This relaxation will sometimes take a conscious effort to produce. Some riders find it advantageous to make a mental check to determine whether there is

---

Remember

1. Sit in the centre of the saddle with your weight equally distributed on the three points of seat bones and crotch.
2. Your legs must lie as close as possible around the horse with the thigh relaxed and the lower legs maintaining a conversation with the horse.
3. The upper body is upright with the head positioned squarely on top of the spine, looking straight ahead between the horse's ears.
4. The upper arm hangs relaxed beside the body, carrying the hands in front of the body with a bend at the elbow. This bend in the elbow enables you to have a sympathetic feel on the horse's mouth.

a particular area in which they have involuntarily become tense. One common area is the nape of the neck and across the shoulders, and relaxation here will often pay dividends throughout the body. The horse will also stay more relaxed if you are relaxed. It will be more sensitive to the demands you make of it and improve the quality of its paces and way of going.

LUNGEING

At whatever standard you are riding it is always beneficial to have some lungeing sessions from time to time to prevent stiffness and/or

positional faults occurring. It becomes especially important if you are training young horses, as you are inclined to get totally involved with what the horse is doing and neglect your own position.

Riding on the lunge under close supervision will enable you to relax and focus your attention on all parts of your body for stiffness or incorrect position. This awareness of how your body is reacting to the movement of the horse will enable you to sit and absorb the movement. It will also help you to apply the aids – the signals you give to the horse – without catching your balance on the reins or gripping with the lower leg.

CHAPTER 4

THE BASIC PACES

There are four basic paces or gaits of the horse in the UK: the walk, the trot, the canter and the gallop.

THE WALK

The horse's natural walk has four beats to each complete stride. This means that it picks up and puts down each foot independently of the others. The sequence of the footfalls in the walk is: near (left) hind, near (left) fore, off (right) hind, off (right) fore. The horse always has at least two feet on the ground.

There are four types of walk – collected, medium and extended, and a free walk on a loose or long rein. In the beginning novice riders will be led at a walk so that they can have a loose or long rein, while holding their balance on the neckstrap. Once they have developed an independent, balanced seat and are confident, they can have the reins. The medium walk and the free walk are the two types discussed here. The collected and extended walk are only used in the advanced training of the horse.

Medium walk
The medium walk must look relaxed yet purposeful. The horse

puts its feet squarely on the ground and moves forwards in a straight line. A novice horse, as with a novice rider, must not be asked to walk on a contact too soon as it can easily spoil its natural paces. Because of this, it is better to allow the novice horse to walk on a long rein in the early stages of its training.

Long rein
A long rein is where the steps remain purposeful, but become longer as you, the rider, allow the horse to take the rein. The horse will stretch its neck down and forwards towards the bit while the rein retains a light contact on the mouth.

Loose rein
A loose rein has no contact on the bit. As a result, the horse has complete freedom of its head and neck and can relax the whole of its spine and swing to the rhythm of the walk. This should be done frequently during a work period so that the horse's neck muscles can relax and allow the blood to circulate. This will reduce stiffness or cramping of the muscles and may lead to less resistance, caused by tiredness, on the part of the horse.

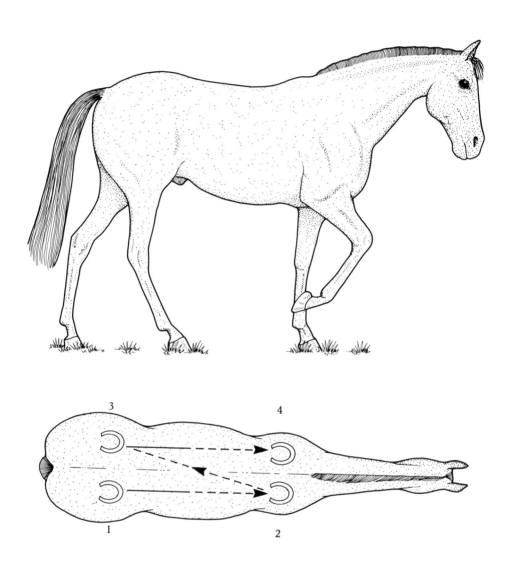

The sequence of footfalls in the walk.

The position

The position at walk remains the same as for the halt, except that you soften the lower back so that it can absorb the movement of the horse.

This is done by keeping the seat bones and the hip joint supple and allowing movement. The upper body stays tall, elegant and in balance. The lower leg remains around the horse ready to apply the relative aids. The arms must hang loosely beside your body with a bend at the elbow and the hands held as though you are reading a book.

Only in exceptional circumstances can the horse extend its toe past a vertical line drawn through its nose. For this reason, to complete a full stride the horse needs to extend its neck and advance its nose past the vertical for each full stride. The rider must accommodate this movement of the head and neck by allowing the hand, arm and elbow to be taken forward by the horse's head and maintaining the contact by returning the forearm and elbow to the original position. This movement must be as if the elbow is lightly sprung, sufficient merely to prevent the rein from slackening between the hand and the bit, thereby making the contact intermittent. In no way must this movement be initiated by the rider. The horse must take the hand and the hand must follow the horse's movement. You must allow, not give and take. This is because the walk and canter are very straight-legged movements, and the horse needs the freedom of its head and neck to complete full, level steps. In trot your hand remains fairly still because the horse bends its knees and does not need to nod its head. Your hand *never* moves up and down.

The elbow is an elastic joint. The rein must feel as though it comes from the bit, through the hand, along the arm, around the back of the shoulders, down the other arm, through the hand back to the bit. Think of it as one continuous piece of elastic that moves sympathetically and in rhythm with the horse. Any stiffness in that circuit can seriously damage the quality of the horse's walk pace. The walk is the easiest of the paces to destroy by bad riding. Restriction in the hand will cause the horse to stiffen in its back and shorten its neck, which will result in the steps becoming short and stilted. Over-enthusiastic use of the leg will push it on too fast, causing it to lose its balance and jog. Riders who stiffen their backs or have an unyielding and hollow back can also cause the horse to hollow its back and shorten its steps.

Remember

1. The walk sequence is near hind, near fore, off hind and off fore.
2. There are four types of walk – collected, medium, extended and free walk (loose rein).
3. Your position remains the same as for the halt except that the lower back and pelvic girdle relax and soften. This allows the body to absorb the movement of the horse.
4. The hand joins the rein to the arm and forms a circuit of strong elastic from the bit, along the arm, around the back of the shoulders, returning down the other arm to the bit. The arm moves sympathetically and in rhythm with the movement of the horse's head.

THE TROT

The trot is a two-time pace – the horse works its legs in diagonal pairs. The sequence of the trot is off hind and near fore together, near hind and off fore together. There is a period of suspension in between as the horse springs from one diagonal to the other – a moment when none of its feet are in contact with the ground. The trot is a lot more bouncy to sit on than the walk, and that is why there are two ways of riding to the trot – the rising trot and the sitting trot. There are four types of trot that can be done by the horse: collected, working, medium and extended. When you have mastered the rising trot, you will find it the more comfortable to begin with.

Sitting trot
In sitting trot your position should remain the same as for the halt and walk. It is difficult in the early stages to keep the seat bones in contact with the saddle. Much of the difficulty arises because riders attempt to hold themselves on the horse's back by gripping with the knee and thigh. This may lead to an even worse fault – gripping upwards with the lower leg and calf. You need to learn to absorb the movement through relaxation and suppleness of the spine and hips rather than fighting against it. You should feel heaviness on the downward movement of the horse's back, rather than grip against the upward movement. During sitting trot it becomes more important and more difficult to keep the pelvic girdle and lower back soft and relaxed. In the beginning you will find it easier to sit to the trot on a horse that does not trot with too much energy.

Rising trot
The position in the rising trot changes slightly. The position of the hip and knee joints must stay supple to allow the opening and closing of the joints as the body rises and lowers. The leg remains around the body of the horse with the thigh relaxed and the lower leg talking to the horse. The ball of the foot rests lightly in the stirrup iron.

Your upper body must incline slightly forward from the hips so that it remains in balance with the horse. In the beginning, it is advisable to have a neck-strap or hold the mane. Your horse should be led at first so that you do not have to worry about control. Before attempting to rise, it is helpful to be able to count out the rhythm of the trot either as up-down or one-two. When you are starting, it is sometimes helpful to practise the action of going up and down in walk to get the feeling of leaving the saddle.

When you start trying the rise at trot, allow the horse to push you up, out of the saddle, on one beat or diagonal, and sit down on the other. At first the action of going up and down seems very small and quite fast.

Once you have mastered a rhythmical, balanced rising trot you then have to learn about diagonals. The horse moves its legs in diagonal pairs. When you sit in the saddle,

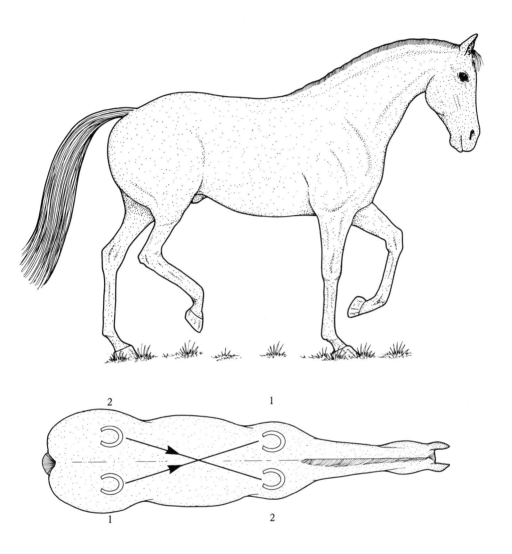

The sequence of footfalls in the trot.

you are said to be on a certain diagonal. If the near (left) fore and off hind are on the ground you are on the left diagonal. If the off (right) fore and near hind are on the ground as you sit, you are on the right diagonal.

It is important to change the diagonal regularly, so that the horse does not become one-sided through using only one set of muscles in its back to push you up in the rise. In addition, if you always sit in the saddle on the left diagonal, for example, the left front leg will eventually wear out quicker than the right front leg.

When you are schooling a horse, it will find it easier to go around a turn or a circle if you are sitting in the saddle as the outside front leg is on the ground. This is because riders can use their inside leg as they

---

Remember

1. The horse uses its legs in diagonal pairs. The near fore and off hind work together, and the off fore and near hind work together.
2. The trot can be ridden either rising or sitting.
3. In the sitting trot, you must sit softly and relax through the pelvis and lower back to absorb the movement. Your position remains similar to that of the walk and the halt. The seat bones should not leave the saddle.
4. In the rising trot, your body changes position slightly. The leg remains in the same position but the body inclines slightly forward from the hip in the rise so as to stay in balance with the movement of the horse.
5. The seat only just leaves the saddle in each rise.
6. Changing the diagonal is important so that the horse does not become one-sided through over-developing one set of muscles in its back; to maintain equal wear and tear on each front leg; to enable the horse to maintain better balance.

---

sit in the saddle to encourage the horse to take a shorter, higher stride with its inside hind leg. This will help it to stay in better balance because its inside hind leg has less distance to travel than the outside one. Apart from helping the horse to develop and balance itself the simple exercise of changing the diagonal increases your ability to discern the movements of the horse beneath you – an ability of increasing importance as your riding education proceeds.

To change the diagonal, you either sit for an extra beat in the saddle, or stay in the rise for an extra beat before sitting.

At all times, your hands must remain quiet, still and sympathetic, and give the horse a good contact on the rein. Your elbow joint must open and close as you go up and down so that the hand *can* stay still. It is also very common to see the rider's legs come away from the horse's sides as they rise. The legs must keep a steady contact and continue a two-way conversation with the horse.

THE CANTER

The canter is a three-time pace with a period of suspension when all four feet are off the ground. The horse should canter with even, relaxed strides, its hind legs well under it to take most of its weight. The forehand should be light and the inside front leg should appear to lead the movement. The sequence of footfalls when the near fore is leading is off hind, near hind and off

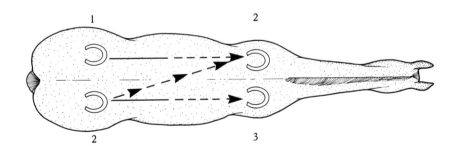

The sequence of footfalls in the canter.

fore together, and near fore. Then there is a moment of suspension before the sequence starts again. The term leading leg refers to the front leg that appears to be ahead of the others. In terms of the sequence, it is in fact the last leg to move within the pace.

When the horse is cantering in this sequence when going to the left, it is said to be cantering on the correct leg and united. If you watch the horse, you will see that the inside legs, in front and behind, appear to be leading. If the lead behind is the opposite to the one in front the horse is said to be cantering disunited. If it is cantering false or on the wrong leg, it is leading on the outside leg fore and hind. However, in certain circumstances as a schooling exercise or dressage movement, the outside lead may be asked for, described as a counter canter.

As with the trot, the canter has four types – collected, working, medium and extended. The working canter is the basic, ordinary canter in which the length of the steps are not as short as in the collected canter or as long as in the medium canter. In the beginning, the canter may seem quite fast, but it is much easier to master than the trot. This is because the movement of the horse is smoother and rounder than in the rather short and choppy movement of the trot. As your body becomes more relaxed the canter will be very comfortable.

When you are feeling secure and

Although the position remains the same as at halt, walk and sitting trot, it is more difficult to remain relaxed and absorb the big movement of the canter.

confident in an energetic trot at sitting or rising, you are ready to try the canter. Your position remains the same as for the halt, the walk and sitting trot, with the hips and back staying as soft and supple as possible. As the canter is a bigger movement, it will be more difficult to remain relaxed and absorb the movement. The canter is also a straight-legged movement, which means that the horse will need to nod its head to complete the stride. Your hands and elbows must allow this movement. You must keep your seat in the saddle for all three beats and keep it still, not sliding backwards and forwards.

The legs must stay relaxed and soft around the horse's sides. If any stiffness creeps into either your lower back, your knees or your thighs, or you start to grip upwards with the lower legs, you will bounce in the saddle. This will be uncomfortable for both you and your horse, and will result in the horse going faster!

Your body should stay upright with your head square on your shoulders so that you can keep in balance and totally relaxed. The waist must not collapse and allow the lower back to become rounded. The upper arm must hang naturally down beside your body, allowing the elbow to follow the movement of the horse's head and neck. Your hand must be sympathetic to the movement of the horse and maintain a light and steady contact throughout each pace.

When you first ride in canter around an arena, keep your weight to the inside, similar to riding a bicycle. Many riders try to counter-balance by leaning out around the corners. This will unbalance both rider and horse, and can be rather dangerous if you fall off between the horse and the walls of the school.

Remember

1. For left canter the horse uses: off hind leg, near hind leg and off fore leg together, near fore leg, followed by a period of suspension. The leading leg is the last to move in the sequence.
2. Your position should remain the same as for the halt, the walk and the sitting trot.
3. The movement of the horse is bigger, so your hips must remain relaxed to absorb the movement.
4. Your hands and elbows must allow the horse to nod its head to complete a full stride.
5. You must ride the horse around an arena with the weight to the inside to keep in balance, like riding a bicycle.

THE GALLOP

The gallop is a four-time pace, meaning that the horse uses its legs separately. The horse assumes a much longer, stretched-out shape and goes very much faster. The sequence of footfalls is: near hind, off hind, near fore, off fore, followed by a period of suspension when there are no feet on the ground. The speed increases with the length of stride and the outline of the horse. You must keep a contact with the horse's mouth through the rein to keep the horse working in balance. You achieve this by using the legs into a steady hand until the required speed is reached.

As the horse gains speed, the centre of gravity moves forward and so you need to move your body into a forward position to remain in balance. The stirrup leather should be taken shorter so that you can bring your upper body forward, with your seat out of the saddle. Your hip, knee and ankle joint have to close into quite a severe angle, and your weight should push down through the lower leg to the heel (the lowest part of the foot). The lower leg remains under you in a similar position to that of the other paces, but with the stirrup leather shorter. Because of the shorter stirrup leather, your seat has to move further back in the saddle to accommodate the knee and thigh. Your hands must be on either side of the horse's neck and maintain a steady contact on the horse's mouth and never be leant upon. On a hard-pulling horse, one hand may be pushed into the neck with a very short rein. The other hand will then give a series of sharp checks with a break in tension in between.

The gallop is an entirely different pace to the canter. Many riders believe that they have galloped when in fact their horse has only cantered fast. Until the pace breaks into four-time it is not true gallop. You will recognize the gallop through the smoothness of the movement of the horse's back and the exhilaration of the speed and power.

Remember

1. The sequence of footfalls is: near hind leg, off hind leg, near fore leg, off fore leg, followed by a period of suspension.
2. The stirrup leather should be shortened, and your upper body folds forward from the hip with the weight out of the saddle.
3. Your angles at the hip, knee and ankle joints become more acute.
4. Your lower leg remains in a similar place but with a shorter stirrup leather.
5. Your seat moves back in the saddle to accommodate the knee and thigh.
6. Your hands stay either side of the neck and keep a steady contact on the horse's mouth through the rein.

CHAPTER 5

THE AIDS

To make the horse understand what the rider wishes it to do in the easiest and most comfortable way has been the aim of riders all over the world for centuries. These wishes are conveyed to the horse through the aids. There are two types of aids, natural and artificial.

NATURAL AIDS

The natural aids consist of the legs, hands, seat and voice. Your legs and hands must co-operate with each other and have the same aim in mind. This means that if you use your legs to ask the horse to move forward your hands must allow it to go forward. To achieve this you must work each leg and hand independently of the others. This takes a lot of practice and cannot be done properly until you no longer rely on the reins to balance.

The legs
The legs lie around each side of the

If the rider uses the legs to ask the horse to go forward but is also restricting that forward movement with the hands, the horse will be uncomfortable and 'natural' movement will be restricted.

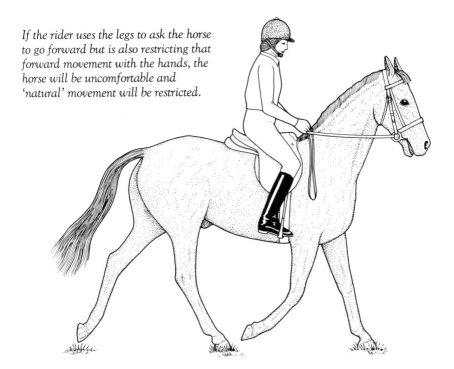

a The horse bending to the left.
b The horse changing its bend as it changes direction.
c The horse bending to the right.

horse with the thigh and knee relaxed. The lower legs are laid in contact with the horse's sides, enabling a conversation each way between horse and rider. The aids are given by the lower leg, on the inside just above the ankle. The aid is given near to the girth by relaxing the knee and closing the lower leg in a nudging movement. The leg must never be clamped on or allowed to flap as this will reduce the sensitivity in the horse's side. Steady use of the leg around the horse will give it confidence and reassurance. Unsteady use of the leg will confuse the horse because you will be giving it continuous messages that you are unaware of, and it will become ultra-sensitive and anxious, especially if all the aids have to be given by the reins. Therefore the leg must maintain a steady contact and give a positive nudge. The way in which the leg is used, and the

amount of leg used, will vary with different horses and situations. Under no circumstances should the leg be raised out of contact with the horse before applying the leg aid.

To ask the horse to walk forward, use both legs at the same time in the region of the girth. Throughout the paces your inside leg should be used on the girth to produce energy. In other words it is the 'stoking' leg. It also helps maintain the bend in conjunction with the outside leg. The outside leg is held slightly behind the girth whenever the horse is on a circle or curve to control the hindquarters. If you want to turn a horse, the outside leg is also brought back to help explain to the horse which way to go.

To ask the horse to go into the trot from the walk, use both legs together in the region of the girth. The aid is very similar to that for the walk transition, but it is used in a slightly heavier, more positive way.

To ask the horse to go forward into the canter from the trot, you should go into sitting trot. Use your inside leg on the girth to keep the impulsion or energy going. Use your outside leg behind the girth to tell the horse with which leg you wish it to lead the canter sequence. The outside hind leg is the first leg that the horse uses to start the canter sequence. Your inside hand bends the horse's head to the direction in which you want to go. The outside hand allows a slight bend of the head and neck and controls the speed when you have got into the canter. For young horses and inexperienced riders, asking for canter in the corner of a manege or corner of a field will make it more likely to be successful than asking on a straight line.

Your horse must be taught from the beginning of its training to move away from the rider's leg and respond to the different signals that are given by the rider. This is so that you can give it secret aids.

The hands

In the main, your hands should follow the movement of the horse's head and neck, and should work as a pair. Your inside hand is responsible for giving directional aids from the fingers. Your outside hand maintains a steady and very secure contact and works in conjunction with the leg aids. Your outside hand also controls the speed of your horse.

The most important thing to remember is that the hand must hold the rein at the correct length and remain sympathetic to the horse. It must *never* be used to

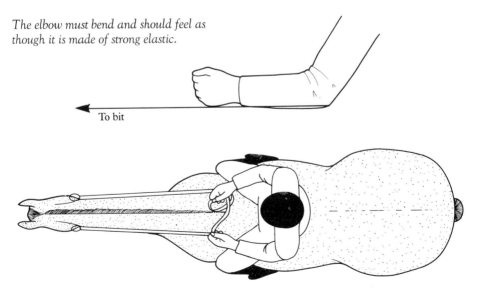

The elbow must bend and should feel as though it is made of strong elastic.

To bit

The hands must remain working as a pair.

punish. Some riders, in their efforts to obtain a good contact, ride on a long rein. This is always a bad rein. Through the inevitable intermittent contact it will jag and bruise the bars of the horse's mouth. In addition, the message given by the hand will take too long to reach the horse's mouth. The weight we feel on the rein contact should feel like a bag of sugar in each hand. The feel must never be 'dead', but springy and elastic. Remember always to use your leg before you use a hand aid. This is to ensure that the hind legs come into action before any movement is executed so that the horse will always be going forward.

Common faults

The legs
1. Stiffness in the knee and/or ankle joint.
2. Gripping with the knee and drawing the lower leg up.
3. The lower leg coming away from the horse.
4. The leg being either too far forward or too far back.
5. It is incorrect to apply a lower leg aid that involves turning the toe outwards and the heel inwards.

The hands
1. The arm being straight and stiff with the hand low and flat, giving the horse a restrictive, unsympathetic feel.
2. The hands not being level.
3. The hands being rough or jerky in the aids.

The horse has a very sensitive mouth and your hands must be sympathetic to prevent it becoming damaged. Your fingers must be closed firmly around the rein so that you have a secure hold without stiffening your arms. When you use the rein to control the speed or come to a halt, you put pressure on the reins. The amount of pressure required will depend on the individual horse. Always think of the sort of feel you are giving your horse. The rein must be held towards the base of the fingers allowing for the natural curve of the relaxed human hand. It is a misconception that the nearer to the finger tips that the reins are held the lighter the feel. Any straightening of the fingers leads to an increase in stiffness of the hand.

The seat
In the beginning, remember to sit as described in Chapter 3 and stay straight. Make sure that your hips and shoulders remain parallel to those of the horse. So, on a circle or bend you must not only remember to change the leg aids into position right or position left but also to turn your body in the direction of the movement. A way to check if you are sitting straight is to make a mental note of how much weight you have in each stirrup and seat bone. If you give yourself a mark out of 10, 10 being heavy, you can then tell if you are level.

The voice
The voice is almost the most important of all the natural aids as it is used to communicate from the

day the foal is born. The horse does not understand the actual words, but works on the tone that is used. It is used sharply with the tone going from low tone to high when an increase in pace is wanted. From walk to trot the voice aid would be 'trrr-ot' in conjunction with a raising of the whip. In the slowing down transition the tone of the voice goes from high to low, saying 'a-n-d w-a-l-k'. The whip is lowered as you use the voice.

The voice is also used when handling the horse in a stable. This again is done from a very early age to warn it of your approach, to move it over, or as a correction. It is vital that it learns to respect you in the stable if you expect it to do as it is asked while it is being ridden. The terms inside and outside refer to the inside and outside of the bend of the horse, which is not the same as the inside or outside of the school or manege.

TRANSITIONS

Any change of pace is called a transition. The success of the transition will depend upon the quality of the pace before it. Before asking for forward movement from the halt you must gain the attention of the horse. The aids to walk on are then given. If the horse ignores the first, polite aid you must repeat it with more determination. The use of the stick will be covered in the next chapter.

When you ask the horse to trot, it must be well balanced and moving forward in the walk with sufficient

---

Remember

1. Your legs and hands must work in conjunction with each other.
2. Your legs must remain in a steady contact with the horse's sides so that they can give a clear nudge when the aid is given.
3. On a circle your inside leg operates on or near the girth to create impulsion.
4. Your outside leg operates just behind the girth to control the hindquarters, and helps to guide the horse in the right direction.
5. To ask the horse to move forward, nudge with both your legs at the same time in the region of the girth. For trot the aid is very similar but is given in a more positive way.
6. To ask for canter use your inside leg on the girth and the outside leg behind the girth. Your inside hand inclines the horse's head in the direction of the movement and the outside hand controls the speed.

To sum up leg and hand aids

1. Your inside leg creates or maintains impulsion.
2. Your outside leg controls the hindquarters.
3. Your inside hand is responsible for direction and maintains a slight bend of the head and neck.
4. Your outside hand allows or denies forward movement.

---

energy. Because the horse assumes a shortened outline in the trot, the rein must first be shortened in order to maintain contact. The leg aids for trot are similar to those of the halt to walk, but are given in a more positive manner. Before making this transition you must make sure that your position is secure enough to stay in balance as the horse increases speed and changes rhythm. It may help you to do the first few steps of the trot in the sitting trot. This will help you to get the rhythm of the trot before trying to rise.

The best place to ask for canter on a named leg is on a 20 m (66 ft) circle at one end of an arena between X and the quarter marker. As you approach the corner, you will unconsciously put your weight slightly to the inside, but you must keep your hips and shoulders square with those of the horse. It is important that you maintain a sympathetic contact on the reins throughout the transitions. If you do not, the horse will just run faster in trot and not canter.

When you are in canter, you must check that the horse is on the correct leg (see page 31). In the beginning you may have to look down to see which front leg appears to be leading. This can be discerned by glancing at the horse's shoulder blades rather than trying to see the actual leg. To see the leg will cause you to lean forward and interfere with your balance and weight distribution.

The gallop is an extension of the canter. The speed increases and the sequence and rhythm change. In the beginning it is advisable to practise the gallop in a large field where the area is enclosed. You use both legs together until the required speed is reached. The hands must keep a steady contact on which the horse can keep its balance.

All transitions must be obedient and smooth, retaining the balance and rhythm of the previous pace. The horse is designed to take its weight on its hind legs in a downward transition, but when it has a rider on its back, the weight on its forehand is increased and the horse's training must compensate for this.

It will be helpful to think of all transitions, upward or downward, as being 'forward'. Never think of coming back to trot from canter or back to walk from trot. The commands should be forward to trot from canter, forward to walk from trot. The hand will restrain the forward movement, producing the decrease in pace, but the legs and in later stages the back will engage the horse's hindquarters.

For all the downward transitions you must sit softly with a supple back and relaxed seat muscles. The legs must be closed around the horse to maintain the impulsion and the forward movement. The horse must never come back or stop dead in a downward transition. The contact must be maintained on both of the reins with the fingers of the outside hand tweaking on the outside rein to slow the horse into the required pace.

It is your responsibility to prepare your horse and yourself so that you are both in the best possible position to execute the transition correctly. For all downward transitions, if you give the horse a half-halt just before the final aid, this will warn it that something is going to happen. The horse will have time to put its weight back onto its hind legs and therefore be in better balance to change pace.

The half-halt is a secret message conveyed to the horse by the rider. It is done by sitting in the correct position on the horse, sitting up and bringing your shoulders back and down. At the same time you close your legs firmly around the horse in a hugging movement and steady the horse on the reins. It must never be done in a rough manner or strongly enough to be apparent to a spectator.

The aids to halt are the same as for any decrease in pace, except that they are a little firmer. As soon as the horse has stopped you must relax so that it realizes it has done everything that was asked of it. It must stand still in the halt with equal weight on all four feet. In a dressage test it must stand square, which means that its front feet must stand in line with each other, with the hind feet also standing in line with each other. When it has halted it must keep standing to attention ready to obey your next command. If your hand aid is used too heavily or held for too long, the horse will try to move about.

Other rider errors in the upward transitions occur if the horse is not listening to the conversation given by the leg, so there is a lack of communication and therefore preparation. If riders lean forward and take the seat out of the saddle they cannot push the horse forward. If the rider has leant forward, very often the reins are dropped at the same time so that the horse will lose its balance and fall into the transition. An anxious or stiff rider may restrict the horse by holding the reins too tight and not allowing it to move forward. All these common faults will prevent the horse from working comfortably and happily. The horse has many different ways of showing unhappiness in its work. It can become over-anxious and nervous, or very sluggish and unwilling to co-operate. It can put its head very high in the air while trying to get away from the bit. If it shows any displeasure, check that you are giving it clear and concise instructions.

The weight of the horse can go forward in the downward transitions. If the rider tips forward or leans back against the horse, this will exaggerate the problem.

TURNS AND CIRCLES

All turns are part of a circle because the horse does not have a hinge in the middle and therefore cannot turn at a right angle. We always speak of 'bending' the horse in the direction in which it is going, which in truth is incorrect. The horse has a rigid backbone and can only contract its ribcage on the inside of a circle or turn and expand it on the outside. By riding a horse through lots of turns and circles we are helping it to become soft and supple and use its body to the full extent of its ability.

For schooling it is advisable to mark out an arena. A small dressage

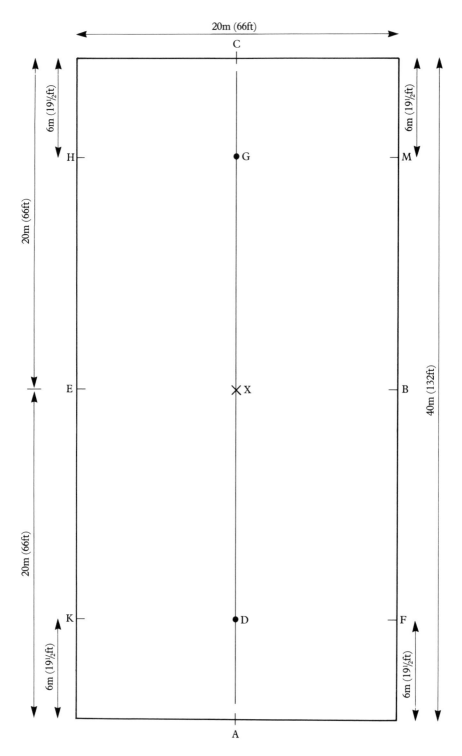

A correctly marked out dressage arena 20 m by 40 m (66 ft by 132 ft).

When riding a circle, think of a diamond shape with the points rounded.

arena is 20 m by 40 m (66 ft by 132 ft) with side and quarter markers. By using an arena, you can tell if your horse is working obediently and accurately.

When riding a circle, always think of a diamond shape and round off the points. This will help the finished shape to be round and of equal size. The aids for turns and/or circles are the same. The inside leg works on the girth for impulsion and the outside leg behind the girth to control the hindquarters. The inside hand is for direction and also helps the bend in the head and neck. The outside hand maintains the contact and controls the pace.

In the beginning, the size of the circles should be 20 m (66 ft), which

Remember

1. The quality of the transition will depend upon the quality of the pace beforehand.
2. In the downward transitions your legs must be closed around the horse to maintain the impulsion and the forward movement.
3. Downward transitions must be progressive so that both the horse and rider can remain in balance.
4. All turns must be ridden as an arc of a circle.
5. Only bend the head and neck enough to see the inside eye.
6. Think in advance of the movement so that you can prepare your horse and yourself sufficiently.

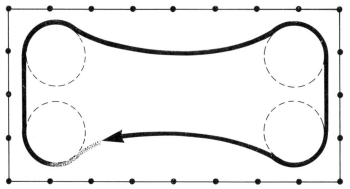

Showing a shallow loop down the long sides of the arena. Small circles can be done in each corner as the horse progresses.

A serpentine of three loops using the length and width of the arena. Again, small circles can be added within each loop.

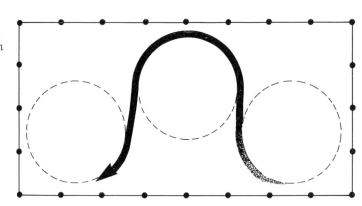

is exactly half the size of the arena. The size of the circles can be reduced as you and your horse progress.

Another suppling exercise is the shallow loop, which is done down the long side of the arena. The horse is bent, for example, to the right through the corner of the arena, you leave the track at the quarter marker and go onto the inside track to a depth of 3 m (10 ft). At this point, the horse is bent to the left and returns to the next quarter mark where its bend is changed back to the right. A circle of 15 m (49 ft) can be added at each end marker to re-establish the horse's balance.

The shallow loop can be developed into a serpentine. You turn the horse across the arena after the quarter marker, parallel to the short ends of the school. On reaching the far track, change direction and just after the half marker turn back across the arena. When you reach the far track change direction again. A small circle within each loop gives a novice horse time to sort itself out.

When riding turns and/or circles the horse must always look in the direction of its movement. If it looks out of the circle it will lean in onto its inside shoulder, which makes it feel very uncomfortable. In fact, if you canter a horse like this it feels like the wall of death! Another common fault is that the horse bends its back too much and then you have trouble controlling its hindquarters. You should only just be able to see its inside eye if you have the correct degree of bend.

Another suppling exercise is to ask the horse to lengthen and shorten its stride in trot. It must maintain a good shape and good balance and just lengthen its stride when asked. Horses that have good movement naturally will find this is a lot easier than those who have not.

Whenever you are riding your horse, you must think well in advance of the movements you want to carry out. You must try and develop a feel for the best time to apply the aids so that they are both sympathetic and effective. Feel and sensitivity are essential to achieve a satisfactory result from your horse. If you are not able to feel how the horse responds to your requests you will miss the little improvements that can cause a great deal of excitement. Some riders have more natural feel than others, but with patience and a generally sympathetic attitude, a sensitive awareness can be achieved.

CHAPTER 6

The Artificial Aids

The natural aids may have to be reinforced by an artificial aid to achieve a result. It is vital that the fitting and use of artificial aids is fully understood so that the communication between you and the horse is improved. If any of them are misused the horse may easily become confused or frightened.

STICKS

There are several types of stick or whip used in the different disciplines. They are of different lengths, weights and diameters. For schooling horses on the flat and for dressage, a long whip is normally used. These can be any length and are used to 'tap' a correction or reinforce an aid behind the rider's leg without the hand being taken off the rein. For show-jumping and cross-country jumping a shorter stick must be used. It must measure between 45 cm (18 in) and 75 cm (30 in) in length overall, and be 1 cm ($\frac{1}{2}$ in) in diameter throughout its length. If the end of your stick becomes damaged or broken, it must be repaired immediately so that it does not hurt your horse. Very often a worn whip, especially the cheaper variety, ends up with the wire protruding at the end, this can cut and cause wounds and should never be used. The best whips are cane, not wire, based. Whereas a dressage whip can end in a braided cord and tassel, a jumping or general-purpose whip should end in a broad piece of leather. The latter results in a noise as well as a slight sting, but cannot cut. The different between these two whips is that the dressage whip is not used as punishment for disobedience but as means of drawing attention to an aid, whereas the jumping or general-purpose whip may occasionally be used in correction or, on rare occasions, punishment.

There are three main uses for a stick: to reinforce a leg aid given by the rider; to teach a young horse to obey the leg aids; and to correct a disobedience. You should carry one at all times. In the first two cases, the long schooling whip is generally used by more experienced riders. However, until you are confident and are able to keep in a good balance, it is better to use a short stick because it is very easy to hit your horse accidentally with a long one. If you do use a long whip, it must not be so heavy that it upsets the balance of your hand, or be too 'springy' so that it taps your horse unintentionally.

The shorter stick is usually used for correction and for jumping. It is also used in showing and racing. If the stick is to be used to reinforce a leg aid, the reins should be put into the opposite hand to the side on which the stick is to be applied. The stick will be used in the same area as the leg aid. If the hand is not detached from the rein, the horse may receive a jab from the hand on its bit. There are, however, occasions when a tap down the shoulder from a short stick, for example when approaching a jump with a less than enthusiastic horse, may be effective. It is very important to become proficient at carrying a stick in either hand. When you ride in a schooling arena it is usual to carry your stick in the inside hand as it is usually the inside leg that needs to be reinforced. Of course, if your horse is hanging on to its friends or swinging its hindquarters out you must change your stick into your outside hand.

When you are jumping it is even more important that you can use the stick equally in either hand. The stick is held with the thicker end between the thumb and the index finger and across the palm, with the thumb pointing forwards towards the horse's opposite ear. The end or knob of the stick should be pushed close to the hand so that there is

little that can poke and hurt you if the horse makes a sudden movement. The narrower part of the stick goes across the palm of your hand with the other end lying across your thigh. Sticks without a knob on the end are very difficult to hold.

Changing the stick from one hand to the other

Changing the stick from one hand to the other must be practised until it becomes an easy, fluent movement that will not frighten or upset the horse. Practise on the young horse so that it becomes used to the movement of the stick without necessarily associating it with use of the stick. The reins must be put into the same hand as the stick and then the short stick can be drawn out from the top by your free hand. You then take it over the withers and pick up the reins into both your hands.

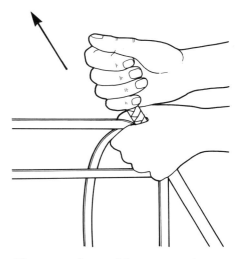

Changing a short stick by using your free hand to draw it out from the top of your other hand.

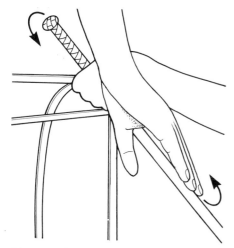

Changing the long stick by putting your right thumb next to the little finger of the left hand, before bringing it over in an arc to the right side.

When you change a schooling whip from the left hand to the right hand, first put both reins into your left hand with the whip. Turn the right hand and take the stick, putting the thumb next to the little finger of the left hand. The wrist of the left hand then twists so the stick makes an arc over the horse's neck coming down on the right side. You can then take the reins into both hands. Practice will perfect this movement.

When the long schooling whip is held across your thigh it is ready for use just behind the leg. Your hand should remain relaxed except for a twisting of the wrist which will activate the end of the whip. If the schooling whip is too whippy there may be an involuntary movement, and this is the reason why a stiff whip is preferable to a floppy one.

If the short stick is to be used in the form of a punishment, you must reverse the stick. This is done by

rotating the stick in the hand so that the end is pointing forward, which allows freer movement of the arm. When you administer punishment you must learn to sit securely in the saddle and keep a firm contact on the reins so that you can control any reaction made by your horse.

The correction or punishment must be given immediately after the disobedience so that the horse is aware of its mistake. You must remain relaxed and calm throughout, because punishment must never be administered in anger. You must *never* use a stick around the horse's head. If you find that you have gritted your teeth during application of the punishment it is probable that you have not controlled your anger and that the punishment may well have been excessive.

The reverse hand-hold of the stick.

The aim of the rider is to become one with the horse.

Riding on the lunge under close supervision, at all levels, is always beneficial.

Left: Rider mounting. Note the toe is
pushed well down so as not to upset
the horse.

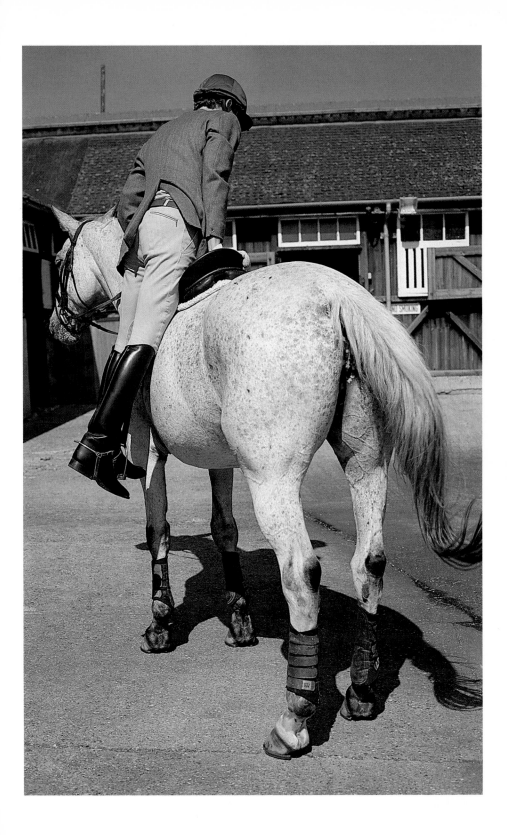

In rising trot the upper body must incline slightly forward from the hips to remain in balance with the horse.

Right: The horse should canter with even, relaxed strides, with its hind legs well under it.

The gallop.

Top right: The horse must be well prepared for a good upward transition from walk to trot.

Bottom right: The horse must be well prepared for a downward transition from trot to walk.

When carrying a stick, the knob must be pushed well down in the hand with the end lying across the rider's thigh.

The spur should be strapped along the seam of the boot so that the knob of the spur faces to the back and is curved downwards.

When without stirrups, the rider must sit deep and relaxed in the saddle.

Top left: The horse cannot focus on the fence when it is very close, so the rider must not interfere with the horse's action in front of the fence.

Bottom left: On take-off the horse will shorten its body and raise its head to lift its forehand off the ground.

Top right: The horse must be able to stretch its head and neck and round its back over the fence.

Bottom right: As the horse lands, it will raise its head and shorten its neck to maintain its balance.

Right: The rider should lower the seat into the saddle for the last three strides so that they can maintain the impulsion, but keep the body angled forward.

Novices approaching a fence should keep the body angled forward from the hip and the seat light.

Above: When walking the course, you must concentrate on the sequence of jumps and how you are going to ride them.

Below: A course of well built fences.

Jumping a grid will build the confidence of both horse and rider at all levels.

The horse turning in mid-air, having anticipated which way it is to go after the jump.

SPURS

Spurs should be used only with caution and only worn by experienced riders who have achieved an independent seat and can easily control their leg movement.

Spurs must be made of metal, and most competitive bodies specify that they must be under 3 cm ($1\frac{1}{4}$ in) in length. Spurs of excessively severe design are not permitted, and the shank must be blunt and under no circumstances have rowels, i.e., spiked wheels. Spurs are used to reinforce the aid given by the leg, as a reminder, and in occasional circumstances as a punishment. As with the use of the stick, they must *never* be used in anger.

The fitting of spurs is vital. Normally one branch of the spur is longer than the other – the longest goes on the outside of your foot, with the shorter one on the inside. They should be strapped along the seam of the boot so that the knob of the spur faces to the back and curves downwards. The buckle must be done up as near to the outside of the spur as possible. Spurs must only be worn when mounted and must always be removed and carried when dismounted.

MARTINGALES

The purpose of a martingale is to lower the head of the horse, and to prevent it from raising its head above the point of control.

The running martingale

The running martingale is the most common type used and is permitted in show-jumping and in the jumping phases of horse trials. It is a leather strap that runs from the girth through the forelegs to the rein, passing through a neck strap at which point it divides into two pieces with a ring on the end of each. The reins pass through these rings. When it is properly fitted it should only come into contact when the horse holds its head too high. It should not break the lateral line between hand and bit when the horse's head is correctly positioned. If you use this martingale, you must have stops fitted onto the reins between the rings and the bit as a safety precaution. They will prevent the rings of the martingale sliding forward and getting caught either on the rein fastening, or worse still a tooth. Either of these will cause the horse to panic and run back at an alarming rate!

The standing martingale

As with the running martingale, the standing martingale is made up of a piece of leather that starts at the girth and comes through the front legs. It remains in a single piece and has a loop through which the cavesson noseband is threaded. It is never used with a dropped part of a flash noseband or grakle. It also has a neckstrap to keep it in place.

It must be fitted so that it only comes into action when the horse raises its head too high. If it is fitted too tightly it will restrict the horse's ability to extend and use its head and neck. This must be remembered if it is to be used for jumping. The standing martingale is an entirely restrictive 'aid'. It is usually used by those who have failed to school their horses properly or have hands akin to dead mutton.

DROP NOSEBANDS

Although drop nosebands are not usually classified as artificial aids they can help with the control of a more difficult horse.

It must be remembered that it always takes two to pull, and that nosebands and martingales are auxiliaries to the bit and can change the action of a bit.

There are several types of drop noseband. All of them are designed to close the horse's mouth and

prevent its jaws crossing. It is important that it is fitted correctly. It must have a broad enough nosepiece so that the pressure is spread over a wider area. It must be about 7.5 cm (3 in) above the nostrils and the bottom end of the nasal peak and the strap fastening under the bit and lying in the chin groove. A drop noseband should have two secondary buckles on the nosepiece so that it can be altered to the different widths of horses' noses.

Flash noseband
A flash noseband is just a strong, padded cavesson noseband with a loop on the front through which another strap is threaded. The loop is fastened below the bit in the same way as a drop noseband. This noseband is permitted for horse trials, dressage and show-jumping.

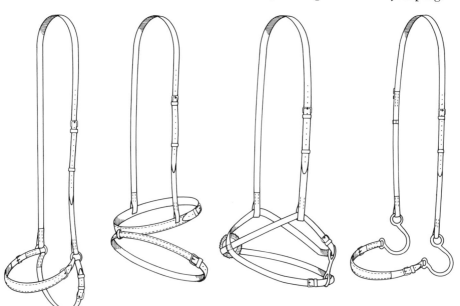

Drop noseband.   Flash noseband.   Grakle noseband.   Kineton noseband.

Grakle noseband

A grakle noseband is a crossed noseband and was the forerunner to the flash noseband. The lower strap fastens below the bit and the top strap above. The pressure is more localized at the point on the front of the nose where the straps cross. It can be adjusted so that the cross-over is higher up the nose, making it more effective on horses that cross their jaws.

Kineton noseband

The kineton noseband is a very severe noseband, and should only be used on very hard pullers. It differs from the other types of drop as it does not close the horse's mouth. It has two metal hoops with a piece of leather connecting them over the nose. The nosepiece is usually reinforced with a strip of light metal and covered with padded leather. The metal hoops fit on the inside of the bit and behind the mouthpiece. When pressure is put on the bit, the hoops are moved backwards and put pressure onto the nose.

Of course, an ordinary cavesson noseband adjusted a hole or two

lower and fastened tight would have the effect of closing the mouth and preventing the crossing of the jaw. If this is to be done, the nosepiece must be padded.

Remember

1. Artificial aids are used to reinforce the natural aids, and must never be used in anger.
2. Sticks come in two types: a long schooling whip, which can be used without removing the hand from the rein; and a short stick, used mainly for jumping.
3. You must practise carrying a stick in either hand and become proficient in changing it from one hand to the other.
4. Spurs must always be correctly fitted and only used with caution by experienced riders.
5. Martingales prevent the horse from getting its head above the point of control by putting pressure either on the reins or the nose.
6. Drop nosebands are designed to close the horse's mouth and prevent the horse crossing its jaw.

CHAPTER 7

PHYSICAL EXERCISES

Physical exercises performed on horseback help the rider in several different ways. They can be done either in a class with several others (which can be great fun), on your own or on the lunge. They improve your fitness by firming up your muscles and making them stronger. This will in turn make it easier for you to control your movements on the horse, and improve your posture. They improve your balance, and as your balance improves your confidence and co-ordination will also improve. When your co-ordination has improved it will make your aids more effective. As your fitness, balance and co-ordination improve, you will be able to relax and allow your seat to become deeper and more secure in the saddle.

The first requirement is to be able to sit deep and relaxed in the saddle and absorb the movement of the horse. The more that the rider tries to hold on by gripping, the more bounce and loss of balance will result. It is not until the ability to relax all your muscles has been obtained that you can pass onto the following exercises.

These exercises need to be done regularly for you to gain the most benefit from them. It is also advisable in the beginning to get your instructor to decide on the best exercises for your particular problems. The demands of the various exercises can be increased gradually as your fitness and concentration improves. You will find that you have muscles that you have never felt before!

As with any riding, and especially when you ride without stirrups, you must be aware of the safety factor. To do any form of exercises your horse must be quiet and have free forward movement. It must be ridden in and loosened up before any work is done without stirrups. It is also advisable to do these exercises in an enclosed space.

When doing work without stirrups, it is more comfortable to have the stirrup and stirrup leather removed completely. This is not always practical as some stirrup-bars are very tight and you cannot get the leathers back on easily! It is more usual to cross the stirrup leathers over the horse's withers in front of the saddle. Before doing this, slide the buckle of the stirrup leather down so that the leather can then lie flat when it is crossed over. If you do not do this it is very uncomfortable and the buckle will bruise the inside of your thighs.

Once you are comfortable, adopt the flatwork position (see page 19). Start by just walking and let the leg relax totally down each side of the horse, having first laid the leg flat on the saddle. Do this by taking hold of the back of the thigh and pulling the muscle to the back. This helps to widen the seat and open the hip joints. The hands at all times must be kept still. As we use our arms and hands to balance ourselves, it is very difficult to keep them still until the hips and the small of the back are supple enough to absorb the movement of the horse. When you first start doing exercises and/or riding without stirrups you must have frequent short breaks. If you become tired and stiff you can do more harm than good to your position.

Having put the leg into position with the muscles in the seat and thigh relaxed, work can then start on loosening the various joints.

EXERCISES ON THE HORSE

Ankle rolling inwards
This is done by rolling the toes inwards towards the horse in a big circle. This will loosen the joint and help 'train' the leg and foot to lie flat and face forward.

Leg swinging alternately
Each lower leg is swung forwards and backwards independently of the other in the motion of walking. This is an exercise to loosen the knees and wriggle the seat down into the saddle. Care must be taken not to kick the horse unless it needs it!

Trunk twisting
First of all put both reins and stick into your outside hand. The inside arm is then raised straight out to the side at right angles to the body. Look at your fingers and turn the whole body to the back so that you are twisting at the waist. This exercise is to loosen the waist and the lower back.

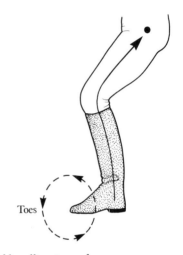

Toes

Ankle rolling inwards.

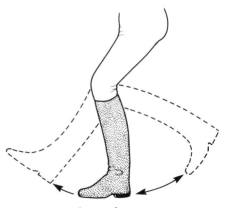

Leg swinging alternately.

Arm circling backwards

Keeping the stick and reins in the outside hand, the inside arm hangs loosely by your side. Lift the arm forward, up and back round in a big circle. This is to loosen your shoulder joints. You must continue to look straight ahead. Across the shoulders past the nape of the neck should remain relaxed.

Arm circling backwards.

Shoulder rolling

The reins can stay in both hands while you shrug your shoulders and roll them backwards. This will have the same effect as the exercise above.

Head rolling

Head rolling is exactly what its name implies. Roll your head around in a big circle, stretching the muscles as you go. Be careful doing this one as it can make you dizzy.

Touching your toes

Again you need to have your stick and reins in the outside hand. You must then bend down with your inside hand and touch your inside toe. Be careful not to let the outside leg slip back as you lean forward to touch your toe. You should also not rest your rein-bearing hand on the neck or withers.

To help with co-ordination you can try arm circling and leg swinging together, or trunk twisting and ankle rolling.

EXERCISES OFF THE HORSE

There are exercises that you can do off the horse to help with the supplying process.

Put the ball of your foot on a raised object, e.g., a fire grate or a tennis ball. Keep the heel on the floor and bend your knee over the toe several times keeping the knee in line with your foot. This will stretch the tendons and muscles down the back of your leg so that it will be easier to lower your heel when riding.

When lying in bed or a warm bath, the natural tendency is to allow the feet to flop outwards in what used to be called the 10 to 2 position. Try to cultivate a position whereby the feet turn inwards. The turning must be initiated from the hip, not merely from the ankle, so that the whole leg turns inwards. This is best achieved in total relaxation, hence the reference to bath and bed.

These exercises should help you

in the ways I have already mentioned and so help you to sit to the trot and canter. When you begin sitting trot you will bounce, especially when you try with your stirrups. Try not to worry about bouncing, but try to do it softly and try without stirrups. Your foot cannot then brace against the stirrup iron causing stiffness in the ankle, knee and hip joint. One exercise I found very useful was to think about rising when I was sitting, making me aware of the rhythm and therefore enabling me to sit softly.

This exercise is especially helpful with the bigger-striding horses. One must relax and lower the leg and absorb the movement by relaxation of the lower back and hips rather than tense the muscles and hold on by grip. The more one can think of heavy legs down either side of the horse to maintain balance and position the better. Any tendency to use grip will inevitably raise the leg and reduce stability.

An exercise which will help you to sit to the canter is to get the horse into canter in the conventional way.

An exercise to help you sit to the canter. Put the reins into your outside hand and put your inside arm across the small of your back and push against it.

Put the stick and reins into the outside hand and put the inside arm across the small of your back. Push your inside arm quite firmly and that will help you to sit into the saddle for each one of the three beats of the canter.

EXERCISES FOR CONFIDENCE

For some exercises that improve confidence and agility, you need a very quiet horse and an assistant to hold it. The following exercises can also be used as races with young or novice riders. They are done without stirrups or reins, which is why you must have a quiet horse with an assistant holding it.

Half scissors
Put your hands, thumbs facing downwards, on the knee-rolls of the saddle. Straighten your arms as you lean forward so they take your weight. At the same time raise and

Safety must be observed at all times, especially when doing physical exercises. Note the assistant holding the head of the horse while the rider does half scissors.

straighten your legs – clap them together above the quarters of the horse and lower yourself back into the saddle.

Scissors

The preparation is the same as above for the arms. When you lean forward, raise and straighten your legs, put one leg a little higher and cross the other one underneath. Lower yourself down into the saddle and you will be facing the other way! To get back again, put your hands flat on the quarters of the horse. You then go through the same sequence and end up sitting where you started – facing the front.

Half dismount

Bring the right leg over the neck so that you are sitting in a side saddle position. Put the left hand on the front of the saddle and the right hand onto the back of the saddle. Roll over onto your tummy letting your right leg slip under the left leg. Straighten your arms and take your weight so that you can lift the right leg clear over the quarters to get back to where you started from. It can also be done to the other side by taking the left leg over the neck.

Round the world

This is another exercise that must only be done on a very quiet horse with an assistant holding it. Put your left leg over the horse's neck so that you are sitting at right angles to the horse's back. The right leg is then swung clear of the horse's quarters bringing you to face the tail of the horse. The left leg follows bringing you facing the near side and to complete the movement the right leg is taken over the horse's neck to bring you back into the conventional position.

This exercise should also be practised in an anti-clockwise direction.

CHAPTER 8

LEARNING TO JUMP

There are two questions you need to ask yourself before you start to consider jumping. Have you acquired a reasonably firm seat independent of the reins for balance? Can you control your horse at all paces both indoors and in the open?

If the answer to either of these questions is 'no', you are not yet ready to learn to jump. Another important factor is whether the horse on which you intend to jump is experienced enough to act as a schoolmaster. If not, you must borrow or hire one that is. Never try to learn at the same time as your horse, it will almost certainly lead to disaster for both of you. Another recipe for failure is to buy a proven performer that is too good for the inexperienced rider. The horse will probably cease to perform and the rider may end up severely frightened.

The best solution is to patronize a good riding school. They will have experienced instructors and reliable horses on which to learn the basics. Having learnt these safely and enjoyably, you will be able to continue gaining experience by practising at home on your own horse. Regular visits to a professional instructor will give you an assessment of your progress and advice on future work.

THEORY OF JUMPING

Before we go on to how to jump, you may find it helpful to understand how the horse jumps.

The horse cannot focus on anything when it is too close unless it tilts its head – when it shies at a piece of paper on the side of the road it puts its head on one side to focus with one eye. So when it looks at a fence, having its eyes on each side of its head, it focuses about 2.8 m (9 ft) ahead. Therefore it is jumping blind for the last 2.8 m (9 ft), so that the last stride to the fence is too late to make any changes. On the approach it sees the fence to be jumped and makes arrangements to negotiate it successfully. During the last three strides, it needs to lower and stretch its head and neck to get its hocks underneath its body so the muscles are ready to lift the forehand on take-off.

On take-off, the horse shortens its neck and raises its head to lift its forehand off the ground, and snaps its front legs up to clear the fence. It then needs to stretch its neck and head out and spring upwards and forwards using the muscles in the hindquarters and back to launch itself into the air. While it is airborne it must be able to stretch its neck and head to their fullest extent and round its back, so jumping with a good bascule; jumping with a rounded back is known as a true bascule. Its hind legs should be neatly folded under it. As it clears the highest point of the fence, its front legs unfold and reach out so it can land with the least amount of concussion, and also allow the hind legs to come down under its body weight. As it lands it will raise its head and shorten its neck to maintain its balance.

When a horse jumps a normal upright fence, not for example a Puissance, it will take off and land an equal distance from the fence, making a semi-circle shape. The horse will measure the take-off from the base of the fence, so the stronger and more solid the groundline of the fence and the closer it is to the ground, the easier it is for the horse to jump. The take-off zone, ideally, is one and a half times the height of the fence away from the base of the upright fence. The more that a fence conforms to the natural flight of the horse the easier it becomes. The triple bar or a 'staircase' fence will be easier for the horse to negotiate, as it fits the curve of the horse's flight, than the upright fence, which does not hold the horse back to its most advantageous take-off point. In contrast, one of the most difficult fences for a horse to jump is a single bar with nothing underneath it from

> ### *Remember*
> 1. The horse cannot focus on anything too close due to its eyes being positioned on each side of its head.
> 2. Coming to the fence, the horse needs to lower and stretch its neck and head to enable it to get its hocks underneath it and its muscles ready to jump.
> 3. In the air it needs to stretch its neck and head and round its back to jump with a good bascule.
> 4. When a horse jumps an upright fence it takes off and lands approximately an equal distance from the fence.
> 5. The horse measures the distance for take-off from the groundline, which should be solid, near to the ground and slightly to the take-off side of the fence.

which it can measure its take-off. Even more difficult, and in some cases impossible, is a false groundline. This is created by putting a groundline on the landing side of a single pole. The horse measures its take-off from what it believes to be the lowest and nearest part of the fence, and will inevitably get too close and knock it down. This situation can be created unintentionally when spare poles are left on the ground on the landing side of a practice fence by inexperienced course-builders. It can also occur when riding in the country. It is important to build confidence over practice fences, and not destroy it with badly built fences or by overfacing the horse.

While not inhibiting progressive improvement, the present capability of both yourself and your horse must not be pushed beyond the limits of confidence. Overfacing can destroy confidence and cause disappointment and dissatisfaction. Keep both yourself and your horse to your own level, where you can get enjoyment from your jumping.

POSITION – ALTERATIONS TO THE FLATWORK POSITION

A good description of a balanced position for jumping is 'being in a position to allow the horse to jump'. Imagine a monkey sitting on your back when you are asked to jump a small fence. If it sits still and in balance with you, you will have a chance to clear it, but if it jumps up and down, or takes a pull on take-off the result would be disastrous! The same principle applies to the horse and rider.

There are several variations on the balanced jumping seat. To begin with, shorten your stirrups one to four holes depending on your length of leg. In the beginning you will only need to shorten the stirrups one or two holes. The important point is to be comfortable. The shortening of the stirrup leather

The basic flatwork position, and the jumping position showing the angles closed at the hip, knee and ankle joints forming the W shape on its side.

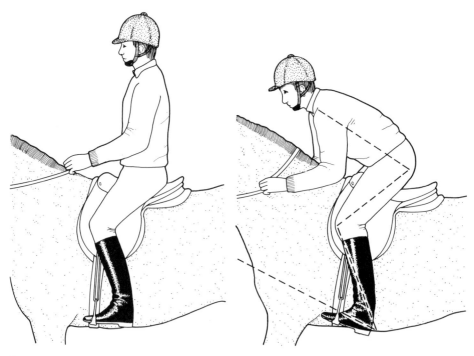

increases the angle in the hip, knee and ankle joints, giving you extra security, which will in turn develop your confidence. You lean your upper body forward from the hip keeping your back fairly flat, making a W shape on its side. On take-off, all these angles need to be closed down to gain the maximum security.

This is the best general-purpose position and the one to be adopted in the beginning. When it has been thoroughly established, slight alterations can be made depending on what the horse is going to do. The horse's centre of balance moves forward the faster it goes, so the rider has to have a shorter stirrup to get further forward to match it.

DETAILS OF THE RIDER'S POSITION

The straight line that you adopted for riding on the flat – between ear, hip and heel – now becomes more or less ear, knee and toe.

The legs

Your legs should remain firm around the horse, with the lower leg in the region of the girth and as much thigh in front of the body as possible. The leg must carry on the conversation, both giving and receiving signals. The rider must also be fit enough that the muscles are strong enough to tighten the knee at the moment of maximum thrust on take-off.

The hip and ankle joints

These must be supple and able to open and close as required. These joints act as shock absorbers and are very important in maintaining the balance required.

The back

Your back should be fairly straight and angled forward, but supple enough to follow the movement of the horse. Your shoulders must also remain square. Good deportment will help produce a good riding position both on the flat and over fences as the back muscles will be properly developed.

The arms and hands

Your arms and hands maintain the straight line from the elbow, through the little finger to the bit and move forward in that direction. The horse can then stretch and use its head and neck over the fence.

A neckstrap or the horse's mane can be very useful to hold onto until you have got used to the feel of jumping, and also on some occasions later on in your jumping career. Allow your hand to be taken by the horse. Excessive thrusting of the hand will cause you to lose your balance and contact. As the neck shortens, the contact is maintained by the elbow returning to its original position. Perhaps the easiest way to understand this movement is to imagine that the elbow is lightly sprung, soft enough to allow the horse to stretch but strong enough to close again maintaining the contact without snatching.

The head

Finally, keep your head up and look forward where you want to go. You will always go where you look, so never look down!

The rider's reflexes

Novice riders over fences should adopt this general purpose position so they can jump small fences easily and learn to follow the movement of the horse naturally. Keep forward and allow your horse to jump. You will learn to feel the rhythm and balance of your horse.

Balance

This is achieved by the rider combining the forward impulsion aids with the steadying aids so that the horse remains light and bouncy, with its weight back, so that it can spring up at the appointed spot.

Impulsion

To keep the horse in balance, the amount of impulsion created by your legs around the horse must be controlled by a series of little checks on the reins. This applies even when you are galloping across country so that the horse keeps its forehand as light as possible.

When you are riding into a fence you must think positively about getting to the other side. Having committed the horse, you must also commit yourself, not be sitting in the back seat!

Seat

Your seat should remain light and forward at the beginning. As you increase your experience and ambition, it can be used to increase impulsion to the fence or to steady the pace, and in turn re-establish balance.

Rhythm

If you count the rhythm of the canter out loud by saying 'canter, canter' or 'bounce, bounce' it will help you to develop the feel of the rhythm. If you can get your horse to come to a fence in a good, steady rhythm and jump out of its stride, you will have a good idea of where it is going to take-off.

Singing a song or counting out loud will also help you to keep breathing normally, which is also very important. Alongside this, you must be aware of your rein and leg contact in order to maintain the rhythm.

Rein contact

Rein contact should be thought of as holding the horse's hand, not restricting but being firm enough. Your arm must remain elastic, with your hands either side of the horse's neck. Never rest on your hands on the horse's neck.

TAKE-OFF

You must incline your body forward from the hip while your hands and legs maintain a steady contact. The angles at your hip, knee and ankle are closed, and you stay in this position, allowing with your hands until the horse lands.

On landing you must stay forward with the horse if you are jumping cross-country. If you are show-jumping, you must gently lower your seat back into the saddle, except when jumping doubles or trebles. With these fences, you should still keep your upper body angled forward at this stage, although when you become more experienced and are jumping large fences you will need to be more upright between the fences. At first, you will not be able to change from an upright position into a folded forward position quickly enough to help the horse, so keep the body angled forward with your seat lightly in the saddle so that the horse can get ready for the next fence.

THINKING AHEAD

When you are jumping, it is very important that you look where you want to go, because the horse will anticipate from the thought and the movement of your weight as to which way it is going. This becomes even more important when you are jumping against the clock, so that your horse lands on the correct cantering leg. If you do not keep

looking for the next fence, especially off a bend, the fences have a nasty habit of not being exactly where you thought they were.

Remember

1. Shorten your stirrups one or two holes, which will close the angles of the hip, knee and ankle joints.
2. The straight line of the flatwork position – ear to hip to heel – becomes ear to knee to toe.
3. Your body must remain forward.
4. Your arm and hand must allow, but only the amount the horse wants to take. Excessive thrusting will push you out of balance.
5. Keep thinking of the rhythm and let the horse jump out of its stride.
6. Always think positively and think ahead.

CHAPTER 9

POLES AND GYMNASTIC FENCES

Before you start any jumping session, there are certain safety rules that you must observe. This applies to any rider at whatever stage they are at. Never practise jumping when you are on your own. Always wear a well-fitting hat with the chinstrap firmly fastened – the jockey skull cap BS4472 or the riding hat BS6473. Wear safe footwear. Use of a back protector is up to the individual rider, but can prevent uncomfortable bruising and/or serious injury.

EXERCISES

The jumping position described in the previous chapter can be practised at any time, even when you are out on a hack. It will help you to become accustomed to the feeling of restriction in the hip, knee and ankle joints. It will also help you to learn to keep in balance with the horse in a more forward position. There are many useful exercises to improve and strengthen the jumping seat. Try the rising trot without sitting in the saddle (warning: do not rely on the reins

for balance). Stay up in the rise maintaining balance independent of the reins, known as the 'vertical high'. Practise the rising trot with the joint angles closed, but without sitting in the saddle, known as the 'horizontal low'. Keep your chest near to the horse's neck but not touching and your back straight not rounded.

All these exercises can cause strain if overdone, especially in the early stages. You should continue with them up to the point when they produce a slight pain in the muscles involved, but should cease as soon as that point is reached.

As the muscles develop, so will your ability to continue the exercises for longer periods.

POLES

Riders and horses practise over poles throughout their careers. In this case, we are going to use poles as an introduction to jumping. They can also be used in the training of a dressage horse who will never jump, to teach it rhythm and balance and improve its stride and impulsion.

Vertical high is an exercise to help the rider maintain balance without holding on to the reins.

At first you will only need one pole. Get forward into your jumping position on the approach to the pole and walk over it. Remember as you approach to keep the horse straight and at right angles to the centre of the pole. The difficult part at this stage is to stay in balance without resting your hands on the horse's neck. When you are happy walking over the pole, try going into trot. Adopt a 'floating

Floating trot is the jumping position without seat contact. Novice riders can use this position on the approach to a fence or over trotting poles.

trot', using the jumping position without seat contact.

In the early stages of using trotting poles, either for the benefit of riders or horses, they should be at double spacing. Use either three or five poles, because horses are always tempted to jump both poles together if there are only two. The distance between them for an average-sized horse of about 16 hands is 2.8 m (9 ft); that is,

approximately three average adult strides. Obviously, if you are dealing with ponies or short-striding horses, the distance will have to be shortened, and larger horses may need a longer distance. With poles spaced like this you can walk, trot or canter over them quite safely.

If you are going to use the poles just for trotting over, they can be set closer together. Set at the distance above, the horse will trot over the

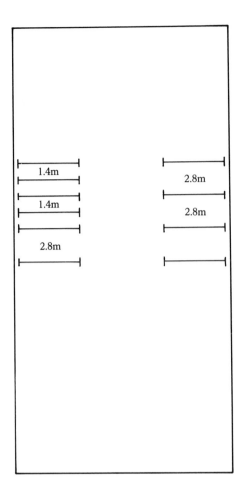

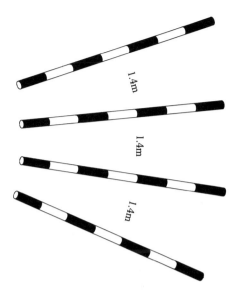

Poles set out in a fan shape.

Poles laid out at single trot spacing left, and double trot spacing right.

pole and then have a stride before the next pole. This gives the horse and rider time to get themselves into proper balance again after negotiating a pole. If using a horse of 16 hands, put your poles at 1.4 m (4 ft 6 in) apart, again making alterations for smaller or larger horses. At this distance the horse just puts its feet down quickly between the poles and immediately picks them up again over the next pole. If you are working with other

people and you are riding horses that are of mixed sizes, you can set the poles in a fan shape. At the narrow end the poles can be set at approximately 1.2 m (4 ft) apart, in the middle at 1.4 m (4 ft 6 in) and a little wider at the other end. These distances should encourage some good trot steps from the horses and also give you more of a challenge in positioning your horse correctly. The approach to the fan should be on a gentle curve matching that of the ends of the poles.

POLES WITH A JUMP

The next progressive step is to combine a small jump with the poles you have been using. It is safer if the poles are pegged in position to prevent them rolling. Cavaletti can

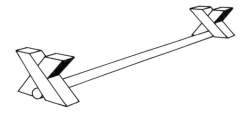

Cavaletti can be used instead of poles, but only in their lowest position.

be used instead of poles, but only in their lowest position. If you are using the poles at double distance, i.e., 2.8 m (9 ft) apart, the fence can also be built 2.8 m (9 ft) from the last pole. If you are using the poles in closed form, your fence must be built at a distance from the last pole of double the trotting pole distance, i.e., 2.8 m (9 ft) (1.4 m/4 ft 6 in is the distance for trotting poles). The fence should start as a very small cross-pole, because a cross fence will help the horse to jump straight and correctly. This in turn makes it easier for the rider to encourage activity and for the horse to jump with agility.

Approach the poles in the forward position, folding forward from the hips, legs firmly around your horse and looking straight ahead. When you are secure in trot over the poles and jump, try one in canter. Either the poles must be set at double distance, i.e., 2.8 m (9 ft), or all the poles except the one nearest to the fence must be removed. Get into canter away from the fence and just keep your rhythm to the spacing pole and jump. Still approach in a forward position.

The next step is to add a second cross-pole, making the beginning of a grid. A grid is a line of fences, from one to four and usually consisting of a combination of poles, to increase the confidence and athletic ability of both the horse and the rider.

When jumping any two fences that are near together, they must be put at a measured distance apart. Of course the surface, terrain and weather conditions will determine the exact distance, but for the average 16 hands horse cantering over small cross-poles, start with a distance of approximately 6.4 m (21 ft). Also remember a downhill slope will lengthen a horse's natural stride and an uphill slope will shorten it. This is so that the horse can take one non-jumping stride between the fences. It may need to be longer for a long-striding horse or shorter for a small horse.

From this beginning you can move on to either more jumps in the line, or putting the cross-poles as straight bars. When you are jumping just two or three fences together, the last one can be made into a spread fence. Keep the front of the fence as a cross-pole and put a single bar behind at the height of the cross.

The distance between the fences can be altered so that the horse puts in one, two, three or four strides between each fence. The bigger the fences go, the longer the distance between the fences needs to be. A rough guide between related fences is 3.65 m (4 yd) per stride. In closely related fences such as combinations a half-stride must be allowed for the

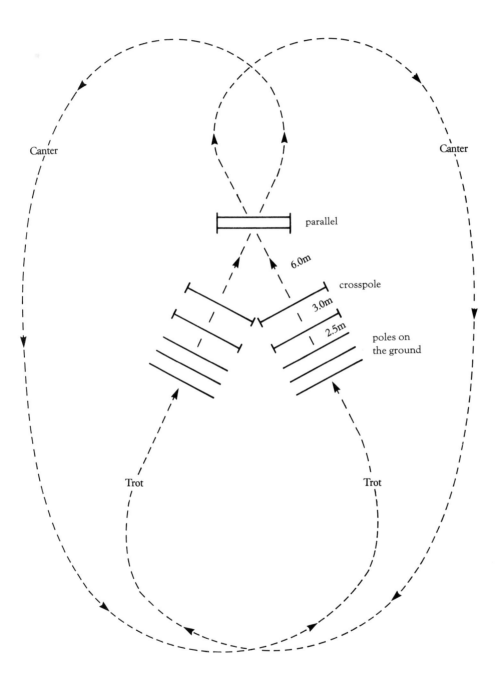

parallel

6.0m

crosspole

3.0m

2.5m

poles on
the ground

Canter

Canter

Trot

Trot

The Iris Kellett pattern.
An ideal gymnastic exercise which will also
introduce horses to jumping on an angle.

horse jumping in and a half-stride for the horse jumping out.

Another exercise that can be done in a grid is known as a bounce. The horse has to land and take off immediately over the next obstacle. Always start this exercise as a pole on the ground followed 2.8 m (9 ft) away by a cross-pole. When the horse is quite happily doing that, make the initial pole into a cross-pole as well.

There are a great number of different gymnastic exercises and grids over which you can practise. One particularly good exercise is to use two cross-poles, one each side of a triangle, as a bounce both going to a parallel, as illustrated in the Iris Kellett pattern on the previous page.

Remember

1. Distances between the poles should be 1.4 m (4 ft 6 in) or 2.8 m (9 ft) for trotting, and 2.8 m (9 ft) for cantering.
2. Keep forward in the jumping position on the approach in the beginning. When you are more experienced you will learn to sit up as you approach.
3. Build the grid up slowly and only make it more difficult when both you and your horse are both jumping confidently.
4. Do not interfere with the horse once you are in a grid, if the distances are right you will meet the take-off zone correctly.
5. Practise the approach from both directions in trot and canter, concentrating on keeping in good balance and a good rhythm.

CHAPTER 10

JUMPING A COURSE

Before jumping a course of fences you must learn to jump single fences. When you were jumping grids, the jumps were set at convenient distances making it easy for your take-off at the exact spot each time. When you come to jump a single fence, it is up to you to keep your horse in a good rhythm and balance so that you come to the fence in a good place for take-off.

It is of vital importance that you keep your horse in a bouncy, balanced, rhythmical canter on the approach to a fence. This will allow the horse to judge its take-off. There are exercises that you can practise to get your eye in so that you can tell if you need to push your horse nearer to the fence or not.

Put down two markers in your training area. Count your canter strides between the two. The second time down shorten the horse's canter by sitting deep into the saddle, holding the horse with the lower legs and giving little checks on the reins. The strides should then be shorter and you will have an extra stride to your original number. Only shorten one stride – two or more are too many. The third time down, lengthen the stride by easing the reins a little and increasing the leg pressure. Your horse will then take one less stride than the original number.

Another exercise is to shout out 'one' as the horse does its last stride before taking off over the fence. The next time count the last two strides – 'two, one'. Go as far back as you can; the difficult part is to count backwards fast.

When you come to jump a single fence, remember that you are the one who has to tell the horse where to go. First of all, get it going forward with enough energy, aiming for the middle of the jump. Any adjustment to the length of the stride must be made earlier than the last three strides. Stay in your forward position with your legs around the horse's sides so you can stay in balance with it as it takes off.

In the air, keep yourself folded forward from the hip with your weight off the horse's back. Do not fling yourself up the neck of the horse as this will throw you off balance. Your weight must be down into your heels and your legs underneath you. Your hands must follow the horse's mouth.

Practise over both small upright fences and spread fences. Having done some grids to begin with, doubles should not cause any problem.

RIDING A COURSE

Riding a course of fences is completely different from jumping either grids or a single fence. It is very important to think ahead all the time so that you get a good approach, take-off, landing and move off. First of all, practise jumping a course at home or hire a set of jumps – never go and jump your first course in a competition.

Warm-up
Warm-up by doing some walk, trot and canter on each rein. Start by trotting your horse over a small cross-pole. Follow this by an upright and a spread fence. Do not jump the practice fence too many times, because otherwise you and your horse will be exhausted before you jump your course, or your horse may become over-excited by repeating the same obstacle.

Jumping the course
Canter a couple of circles and when you are ready make a wide arc to the first fence. Ride it in the same way as you have ridden the single fences. Keep the horse straight, fold forward, put your legs on, allow with the hands and look straight ahead. Keep your horse in a good, bouncy, rhythmic canter and pick this rhythm up again after your jump. If you have to change direction during the course, get the horse onto the correct canter lead as soon as possible. If there is not room, just keep your horse in balance and keep moving forward. Doubles are to be ridden just as if it was one of the grid exercises.

COMPETITION RIDING

You will walk the course before you ride your horse around it. Make sure that you know where the start is positioned and how far away it is from the first fence. See if it is jumped towards or away from the collecting ring or horse-box park. Horses live naturally in herds and like to be together, so jumping away from the collecting ring will be more difficult than towards it.

See how tight the turns are into the fences, and what type of fences they are. Brightly coloured jumps or spooky jumps need to be ridden more positively than a rustic or a straightforward pole jump. In competitions where a jump-off will be decided against the clock, the optimistic rider will also walk the jump-off course, working out the time-saving routes and turns.

You should use the warm-up period in exactly the same way as if you were at home. The only rule you must observe is that the practice jump will have to be jumped from one direction only. Always keep the red flag or red wing on your right and the white flag or wing on your left. This is to prevent people colliding.

When you enter the ring, canter around the jumps until the bell rings. Do *not* pass through the start, even on your warm-up circle, before the bell rings. Once it does ring, you can start. When you have passed through the start, your round has officially begun so just keep your horse cantering from one fence to the next. Never look round if you hear a bump behind you, because you may miss the next fence as well. You can always find out what the noise was when you have finished your round. Always go through the finish. Get off your horse as soon as you are out of the ring and make much of it.

Remember

1. Keep a bouncy, balanced rhythmical canter on the approach to the fence.
2. Aim the horse at the centre of the fence.
3. Practise over single upright and spread fences.
4. Do not over-jump your horse in the practice ring.
5. Practise a course at home.
6. In competition, walk the course thoroughly.
7. You have started as soon as the bell rings.
8. Never look back – whatever the noise!
9. Always go through the finish and do not dismount until you have left the ring.
10. Always dismount after leaving the ring, and do not use your horse as a grandstand.

EQUIPMENT REQUIRED FOR BUILDING FENCES

When learning to jump, a full set of beautifully painted jumps would be ideal, but they are not absolutely necessary. All you need to begin with are some poles of 3–3.65 m (10–12 ft) long. If you are using proper jump standards, the metal cups must be removed if they are not holding a pole. Spare poles must be laid away from the fence so that your horse cannot step on them, or you fall on them, if the horse refuses the jump.

Many simple materials can be used to make interesting jumps at little expense, but do always be aware of possible danger. For example, straw bales can make very good, solid-looking fillers for jumps, but lie them so that the strings are not visible. A horse can get its foot stuck with the string between the foot and shoe and then panic – causing it and you to become very frightened. Bales should be topped with a pole.

When making a water ditch, a piece of board painted silver will give a very good effect. Walls and fillers for fences can be made out of boards or old doors. Remove any catches and then paint them. Good quality oil drums, rubber road-cones and fertilizer bags all make excellent fences. If tyres or oil drums are used, they must be secured so that they cannot roll, and positioned so that the horse cannot get trapped in them. Sawn-up wooden pallets can make very adequate stands.

Do not forget that the countryside also provides some very interesting natural obstacles. Riding up and down hills and slopes can strengthen your position and improve your balance. Riding through fords, first making sure that the bottom is safe, will improve the confidence of your horse in water. Having got the permission of the farmer first, and checked that there is no wire, you can look out for suitable hedges, rails and ditches. Interesting fences can be made out of everyday things such as a garden seat. If you are tempted to use a table, it must be reinforced on the top just in case the horse tries to bank it, i.e., land on top and take off again.

BUILDING FENCES

It is important to build confidence over practice fences, and not to destroy it by using badly built fences or overfacing the horse. Bear in mind that when you are jumping an upright fence, the horse will take-off and land an equal distance from the fence.

A hogsback The take-off side has a low rail and the middle rail is the highest point. It has a lower rail on the landing side.

A triple bar is built into the natural jumping shape of the horse. It has three ascending rails, making a staircase profile.

An ascending parallel Another type of easier fence. The front rail of the fence is lower than the back.

A true parallel The back rail is only just visible to the horse on take-off. This fence is extremely difficult as the horse has no time to make an alteration to the shape of its jump.

When jumping any spread fence, the back element must have only a single pole, with nothing underneath it. The front element of all spread fences should be filled in with either poles or a solid filler such as straw bales. With a triple, the slope must be constant and the centre pole must touch a stick laid from front to back. Should there appear to be a hole in the middle, a second pole or filler can be used underneath it.

Each obstacle should look well filled in. It should have a solid appearance with a well-defined groundline slightly in front of the fence. Remember that no groundline, or a groundline set behind the front of the fence, make it extremely difficult to jump.

To negotiate a spread, you must make height. Over a normal fence, discounting specialist fences such as Puissance, the horse will take off approximately one and a half times

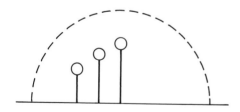

Triple bar.

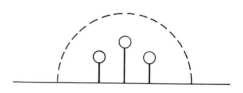

Hogsback.

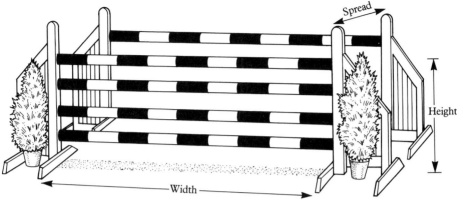

True parallel.

the height of the fence away from the fence. For example, over a 1.2 m (4 ft) upright it will take off approximately 1.8 m (6 ft) from the base of the fence and land approximately 1.8 m (6 ft) away from the base, a total spread of 3.65 m (12 ft). It therefore follows that the best way to jump 3.65 m (12 ft) of water is to imagine a 1.2 m (4 ft) fence in the middle of it. When you teach a young horse to jump

water, always put a small, solid-looking fence on the take-off side and a rail over the centre of the water to maintain the height of the jump. There is no need to gallop flat out into a water jump because the horse will only flatten its back. If it clears the water it will probably hit the next fence.

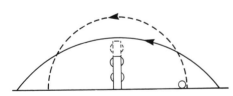

Over a normal-sized obstacle the horse will take off from a point in front of the fence approximately equal to one and a half times the height of the fence. When the fence is very big, i.e., Puissance, the horse will get closer to the base of the fence.

Remember

1. You must build fences to build confidence and not destroy it.
2. When a horse jumps an upright fence it will take off and land an equal distance from the fence.
3. Easier fences have lower rails at the front than at the back.
4. More difficult fences have the front rail the same height as the back rail.
5. The groundline of a fence must be solid and slightly in front of the fence.

CHAPTER 11

COMMON CAUSES OF BAD JUMPING AND REFUSALS

There are numerous reasons why a horse refuses to jump a fence, and they can range from being naughty, to fear or lack of confidence in the horse or rider. It is important that the cause is identified so that the right correction can be made.

REFUSALS – THE HORSE

A young or novice horse will naturally be suspicious of new fillers under fences, ditches and water, and jumping into dark places. One solution is to use one of the horse's natural instincts, by having an older, more experienced horse jump the obstacle first. The nervous horse will then gain confidence from following the lead. Once it has realized that there is nothing to worry about, it can then try it without a lead. The lead horse should, however, in the first few instances be halted on the landing side of the fence as an enticement.

When horses are jumping courses they can sometimes lose confidence over combinations. If they creep over the first element, which makes them land too near to it, there will be too much distance to be made up to jump out easily. On the other hand, if they over-jump the first element and land too far into the combination, they will not have enough room to jump out easily. Gridwork over small fences set at related distances will help improve both of these problems.

The terrain and conditions underfoot can make a tremendous difference to the performance of your horse. It can lose confidence very quickly if the going is slippery. If you have ever tried to run down a slippery path you will appreciate how insecure you can feel, and that is without having to negotiate a fence in the middle! The worst kind of slippery going is when the ground has become hard and dried out and then has a shower of rain on top. Worn shoes without any grip left on the bottom can also be slippery, and coupled with hard, damp ground they can spell disaster.

Studs

I advocate the use of studs and usually have them in all four shoes. I put one in the outside of each front shoe and one on each side of the hind shoe and use them for both dressage and jumping. I have small, pointed studs, called ice studs, in the front shoes and larger ones in the back. On hard ground I use the medium-sized stud and only use the large square ones for wet going. Experience will help you decide which ones are best for your particular horse.

When you have put studs in your horse's shoes, you must keep it on soft going otherwise you will unbalance its foot, causing strain on its joints. After working your horse, remove the studs, put some grease into the hole and then fill it with cotton wool. The hind shoes can have small mordax road studs put in the holes instead of the cotton wool. This can make it easier to put the studs in next time.

Surfaces

If you are working on a prepared surface, you will not require studs. Some surfaces can be loose, so they move when the horse wants to take-off. Others are too deep and hold the horse at the moment of take-off. Do not jump from a prepared surface unless it is firm and well settled. Remember that the fences will be about 7.5 cm (3 in) higher when jumping from a loose surface.

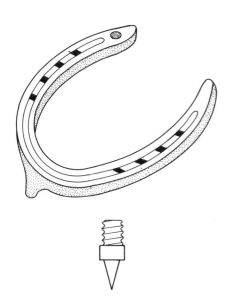

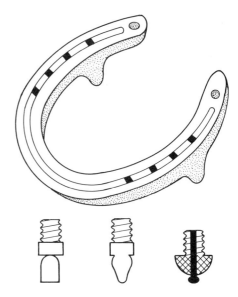

Front shoe showing the stud hole and a pointed ice stud.

Hind shoe showing the two stud holes and working hind studs. The shaded stud is a mordax road stud.

RIDER ERRORS

As previously mentioned, you must always ride over the fence, not just to the point of take-off. You must ride with confidence and determination, dropping down into the saddle just before take-off and increasing the leg contact. Although you must allow the hand to follow the stretching of the horse's neck, you must not remove the contact just before the fence. This fault is called 'dropping the horse' and is exactly what the saying implies. Imagine you are holding a rope and it suddenly gave, you would fall over. The same would happen to the horse. If it has a steady contact on the rein and it suddenly goes, the horse will fall onto its forehand and either stop dead or stumble over the fence. Equally, it is impossible to 'lift the horse' by taking on the rein on take-off. This just distracts the horse's attention and restricts the movement of its head and neck, i.e., its balancing pole. The bouncy canter that is full of impulsion and the straight line to the centre of the fence has already been covered quite fully in previous chapters. It cannot be stressed enough that a poor approach, a wrong angle or a half-

'Lifting' the horse.

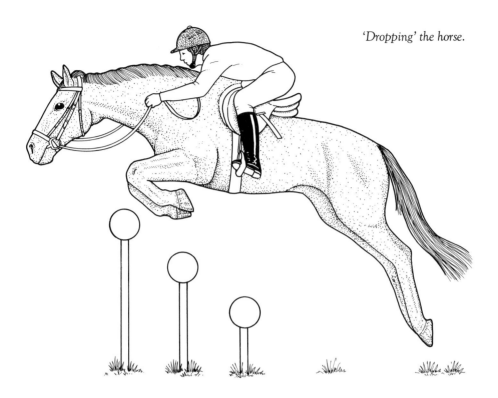

'Dropping' the horse.

hearted rider will ruin any chance that the horse may have of jumping successfully.

DISOBEDIENCE

Treatment of any form of disobedience must be according to the reason behind it. Before you start jumping the horse must be obedient to your leg and steering aids so that you maintain control and present the horse correctly to the fence.

Bad presentation
This is usually due to poor riding, or to disobedience to the aids. You must look for the fence in plenty of time so that you can judge the distance and keep your horse in a good balance. When you are turning into the fence, your inside hand must not pull the horse round and restrict its use of its shoulders. Remember your leg aids, and ride the horse around the corner with a strong outside leg.

Running out
The horse runs past the fence, having set its jaw and led off with its shoulder. When a horse refuses a jump by stopping in front of it, it has generally said a definite 'no'. A run-out usually happens because a cheeky horse takes advantage of a weak or complacent rider. It has not said a definite 'no', but a 'perhaps not'. Generally speaking, a positive rider who can keep the horse

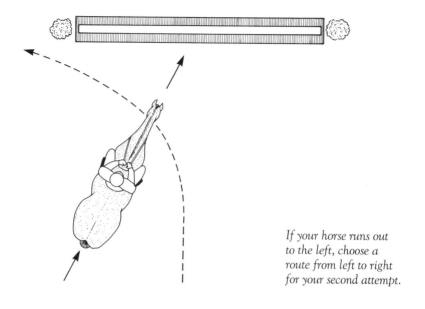

If your horse runs out to the left, choose a route from left to right for your second attempt.

straight will stop the horse running past. If a horse runs out to the left, stop it and turn it to the right so that it cannot just keep going around on a circle. You will score a moral victory by turning it right. If your horse has run out to the left, and does this habitually, do not approach the fence on a straight line to the centre but choose a route from left to right. The horse, following its inclination to run out to the left, will then find itself confronted by the centre of the obstacle and will accept the necessity to jump. Obviously the horse that runs out to the right must be steered from right to left. Always remember that prevention is better than cure, and if you abide by the rules of good presentation and determination, and introduce new fences carefully, the problem should not arise.

Rushing

This is a lack of control on the approach to a fence. It can be an acceleration in the last few strides or a mad dash from a distance away from the fence. It is the effects caused by rushing that are dangerous, not the actual rushing. Rushing can result in either an unbalanced jump, a fence down because the horse has flattened its back and dropped its legs, or even a fall. Probably the most frightening result for the rider is if the horse suddenly realizes that it cannot jump the fence and puts in a sudden stop. This type of refusal is particularly unseating for the rider.

A horse that tears round a course, completely out of control, is not necessarily enjoying itself. No horse is born to rush. The horse in its natural state relies on flight to run away from perceived danger or

The rider lacks control on the approach to a fence, and the horse rushes at it.

frightening experiences. The fact that the rider directs it towards the frightening object, that is, the jump, does not stop the flight. So the rushing horse may well be rushing towards what frightens it. The reasons for its fear might not just be the fence's dimensions. It may be caused by the unsympathetic hands of the rider, injudicious use of the whip, unsuitable bitting or physical pain due to injury or strain. Sometimes a horse will try and go too fast because it is over fresh, and may also buck on landing. This is usually a short-lived problem because as the high spirits disappear, the problem will also disappear. Over-excitement may be caused by an excess of 'intoxicating' feed such as oats.

Spooking

A horse looks at something as if it has ghosts around it. Some very good horses will spook at a piece of paper on the side of the road, but then jump a fence with plastic bags underneath it without turning a hair.

The problem arises when a horse spooks at a fence and therefore loses impulsion and all forward movement to the fence. This will cause it to shorten its stride and jump in a crooked, uncomfortable manner. When your horse does this, it is very difficult to maintain a fluent, rhythmical stride because it drops the bit and stops going forward. Young or inexperienced horses can be very spooky and should not be ridden by novices. Horses that continue to be spooky after receiving a certain amount of

training are not suitable as competition horses.

Practise your horse over small, spooky fences, maintaining a good rhythm and straight approach by positive riding. Never chase your horse over a fence.

Strong, pulling horses

If the horse leans on your hands and travels too fast, it will jump flat and trail its hind legs. If the horse is strong in your hands, it is relying on you for balance and support and its weight will fall forward on to its forehand. This makes it difficult for the horse to make any adjustments as it approaches the fence, and for you to keep it in balance. Lack of training and discipline are the most common reasons for lack of control. If the horse is on the forehand, this must be corrected by schooling on the flat.

It is important that you are able to differentiate between whether a horse is strong, evading the aids, leaning on the forehand or rushing. When you have diagnosed the problem, you can begin the rehabilitation period. Before increasing the severity of the bit, it may be advisable to try something milder. The horse could just be running away from the bit and/or the rider's hands.

Overfacing

A horse is asked to jump fences that are outside its scope or stage of training. This may result in it having a bad experience or a fall at the fence, which will cause it to lose its nerve. If the horse becomes frightened at any stage of its career,

Overfacing either the horse or rider.

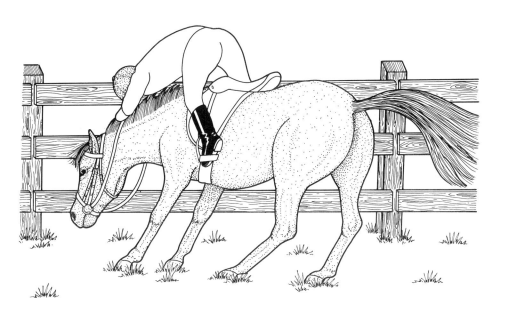

it must be taken back to smaller, easier fences until it is confident again. The rider may also be overfaced and be driven by ambition rather than ability. It is unwise to rely on the resolution and courage of the horse to substitute for the deficiency of the rider.

If your basic training has been correct there should be no reason for lack of confidence or fear when the horse is jumping.

DISCOMFORT

Another cause of fear in the horse is any pain it may feel when jumping. Bad or inexperienced riding can give the horse a jab in the mouth, or the rider's weight may come heavily down onto its back. There are other problems that can cause pain, and which can be put under the heading of minor ailments.

Teeth
The action of the horse chewing and the fact that the upper jaw is wider than the lower jaw cause the teeth to become razor-sharp. They can cut large holes in the cheeks or the tongue, causing the horse great pain, especially if you then fit it with a tight noseband because it has become strong. The teeth must be checked every 6 months at least either by your veterinary surgeon or a properly trained equine dentist.

Bitting
As previously suggested, all novice riders should use a snaffle bit. A strong bit coupled with

Using a strong bit coupled with inexperienced hands can spell disaster.

inexperienced hands can stop a horse dead or cause it to run away.

Pain in the back

This may stem from a number of different causes, and will make the horse reluctant to jump. Advice on back problems should be sought from veterinary surgeons with specialized knowledge of chiropractic. Pain from lameness in the foot or legs can cause a horse to refuse to jump. In some cases a drop in performance can indicate a veterinary problem.

Weakness and lack of condition

Your horse must be kept healthy by correct feeding for its type, size and the work it is expected to do. It must also be wormed every 6 to 8 weeks so that it can get the most out of its food. Grooming and regular care of its feet by the blacksmith are all part of the general care you must give your horse.

Jumping must be a continuation of your flatwork, maintaining the balance and rhythm. Rushing is usually due to a mental block and takes time and patience to rectify. Return to the use of trotting poles, and build grids with solid fillers to get the horse to 'back off' and slow itself down. You must resist getting into a pulling match against your horse. Working the horse among fences without jumping can sometimes help to relax it.

Remember

1. Confidence can be improved by gridwork, and by taking a lead from a more experienced horse. Enticement should be provided on the landing side of the fence, and can take the form of non-jumping members of the ride, the stables or the horse-box.

2. The use of studs will help the horse to maintain its balance on slippery ground.

3. The rider must be responsible for the approach, the balance of the horse and the angle to the fence so that the horse has a chance of jumping successfully.

4. A horse runs out at a fence because either it has taken advantage of a weak or complacent rider or it has been presented to the fence badly.

5. If a horse rushes, it is more likely to be anxious about jumping than 'enjoying' its jumping.

6. Pain can cause the horse to refuse, and may be related to minor ailments or management problems.

When you are riding uphill, lean slightly forward over the shoulders of your horse.

CHAPTER 12

PRACTICAL HINTS

It is important that you learn to ride outside as well as inside, because not only will it provide the opportunity to explore many different types of terrain, but it can also be very exciting or relaxing. Horses react in different ways when they are outside the confines of a school or arena. It is important for your own safety, and that of others, that you can control your horse easily and confidently. When you are riding out, it is vital that you remain alert and ride properly at all times.

HILL WORK

When you are riding uphill, lean slightly forward over the shoulders of your horse. This takes your weight off its back and reduces the strain on the hindquarters.

When you are coming downhill, especially if it is steep, you must keep the horse straight. The direct route is always the safest, as the horse is more likely to slip or trip if taken down at an angle. Sit as tall as you can but do not lean back, and keep your weight down into your legs and heels. Keep a contact on the horse's mouth but allow the horse to use its head and neck to balance.

Hill work is very beneficial to the development of the horse. It will improve its strength and endurance, and is used especially in getting horses fit. Cantering a horse uphill will make it use its muscles and lungs to the maximum limit building up their working capacity.

CONTROLLING A STRONG HORSE

If you find that your horse becomes strong when you are cantering in open spaces, you must not just lean back and pull against it. This is both ineffective and rough. The horse is so much stronger than we are that we have to be much more subtle in our approach.

One way to control the horse at the canter or gallop is to bridge the reins. Have the reins very short, and keep the reins in both hands. Then turn your hands flat and take the spare end in the left hand. You then put the reins onto the horse's neck and brace them just in front of the withers. Even if the horse pulls, it cannot pull the reins out of your hands because it is pulling against itself. This method is used by jockeys galloping racehorses to keep them under control and in rhythm. If you need to stop, you should use the next method.

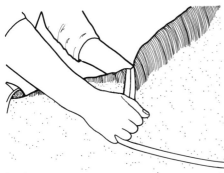

Bridging the reins.

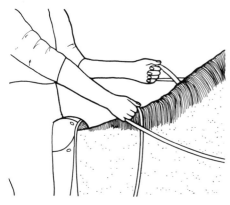

To stop a galloping horse fix one hand with the rein short onto the neck and take short, sharp checks on the other rein.

Keep your position in the saddle stable and anchor one hand, with the rein very short, into the horse's neck. Give a series of sharp checks on the other rein. If you pull on both reins continually, the horse will just pull harder and can usually go on for longer than you can.

If you are riding in the countryside, you must observe the Country Lore.

Woodland

Allowing your horse to nibble or tread on young trees, the breaking down of the edges of ditches and the disturbance of game will all cause unnecessary damage, and annoyance to landowners and gamekeepers. Always keep to the tracks and ride slowly and quietly so as not to disturb the game.

Farmland

If you are going on private farmland you must first gain permission from the farmer and follow his instructions. When going across farmland it is important that you know if the field has been ploughed, drilled and/or harrowed. Unless otherwise instructed, always keep to the headland around the edge of a field and *never* go on the crops.

If you go through a grass field with stock in it, always *walk* through. *Always* shut closed gates after you or leave open gates open, and *never* damage the fencing. Always speak to people who work on the farms so that you create a friendly situation. You should not speak to strangers, but it is important to be polite and courteous at all times, and always speak to anyone you know – hopefully this includes the farmer.

When you are mounted, you are allowed by law to ride along bridlepaths. You must proceed at a sensible speed and be polite to other users. You have no right by law to use footpaths.

OPENING AND CLOSING A GATE

Stand your horse parallel to the gate with its head facing the latch. Put

Opening a gate.

Always be courteous to those who show consideration to you.

your reins and stick into one hand and with the hand nearest to the gate, open the latch. Use the leg nearest to the gate to push the horse away from it and you will then be able to open it. Make sure the gate is open wide enough to allow the horse to get through without catching you or itself. When you are through, bring your horse parallel to the gate again so that you can close the gate and fasten the latch with your free hand.

RIDING ON THE ROAD

As always, you must wear a hat that meets the legal safety standards. If you are riding a young horse, you can purchase a bib with 'Young Horse' written on it. If you ride in bad light, you must ride in reflective clothing. A safety lamp must be fitted to the offside stirrup and the horse must have reflective bands on its legs.

When you are riding on the road, look, listen and think ahead at all times. You must follow the Highway Code just like other road users. It is advisable to have a third party legal liability insurance as the rider of a horse can be considered liable if the horse causes damage or harm to other people or their property.

Always show consideration to all other road users. Pedestrians may be frightened of horses, so always pass them at walk. A friendly greeting may reassure them. Always smile and thank anyone who slows down or shows consideration to you. To thank a driver, put both

reins into your left hand and raise your right hand and smile.

Do not venture out on to the road on a strange horse on your own. Always get a friend with an experienced horse to accompany you. A young horse can be turned out in a field near to a busy road to help acclimatize it to traffic. When it goes on to the road for the first time, take an experienced horse between you and the traffic. The young one can then be protected from the traffic by its escort. Traffic-shy horses often have traffic-shy riders who transmit danger signals to their horses through their own tension.

Signals must be given early and in a clear, decisive manner. For left and right turns, the arm should be fully extended with the hand flat and the fingers closed. Before you give your signal always look behind and look again before turning. The fact that you have signalled will not automatically guarantee your safety.

When you are turning to the right at a T-junction, never stand in the middle of the road as cars will then come up each side of you. Stay on the left-hand side of the road and when·it's safe cross *straight* over. If you are in doubt, wait.

If you wish to slow a vehicle down as it is approaching, put your reins and stick into the left hand. Extend your right arm to the side and wave it slowly up and down.

Hazards
There are many hazards to be encountered when riding out of doors. If you approach noisy machinery try to catch the attention

of the operator so that he will switch it off. If he does, always thank him. If there is something frightening ahead, do not try to pass it if there is traffic all around. Wait until the traffic has passed and then go ahead. Never dismount as the horse may jump sideways and cause you injury and then escape and cause further accidents.

If a very large lorry approaches from behind, keep the horse tight to the left-hand side of the road by using a strong right leg. Turn its head slightly to the right so it can see the lorry. The same action must be taken if the horse shies. If you use the left rein, the horse will think you want it to go nearer to the object and shy further away from it. If you have hold of the left rein, its quarters will swing out into the road and it will escape through its right shoulder. You must 'shut the door' by using your right leg strongly and holding the right rein. By doing this you have blocked the horse's outside shoulder.

Ride on grass verges whenever it is practical. Do not canter on them as this can be dangerous. Never ride on ornamental verges or private lawns. Some local authorities have by-laws that forbid the riding of horses on verges, so check whether this applies in your area.

With the amount of traffic that is on the roads nowadays it is not advisable to ride one horse and lead another. However, if you have to ride and lead, always ride on the left-hand side of the road with the led horse on your left, away from the traffic. The led horse must always have a bridle on with the reins over its head, correctly held.

When riding in groups, you should take extra safety precautions. A group should never exceed eight in number, and should ride in pairs. It should be escorted by two experienced people, one at the front and one at the rear. Road signals are given by these two riders. To make it easier for traffic to overtake, the group may be split into two groups with 100 m (109 yards) between them. If the group behind become upset, it would be sensible to keep everyone closed up.

The leader of the group must set a pace that all the members of the group can maintain safely and comfortably. In heavy traffic it may be more sensible to ride in single file. If this is necessary, you must decide beforehand who is going in front and who behind. It is obviously much better to ride out in smaller groups or pairs.

Before you leave the yard, always inform someone where you are going and approximately how long it will take.

If you or one of your friends is unfortunate enough to have an accident, something has to be done immediately. If the accident happens on the road:

1. Send someone ahead and behind to warn oncoming traffic.
2. Go to the patient and reassure them, making a calm examination of the severity of the injuries.
3. Get someone to summon an ambulance and the police.
4. Instruct someone to catch the loose horse.

If a horse shies at something on the verge, keep the outside rein firm and use a strong outside leg. This will prevent it from swinging its hindquarters into the road or escaping through its shoulder.

The BHS issue an accident procedure that will apply to most accidents. When you are carrying out these actions, remember that your safety is of paramount importance, so do not take unnecessary risks. As for all road users, a basic knowledge of first aid treatment can mean the difference between life and death for you or your friends.

Remember

1. Hill work will help develop the muscles, strength and lung capacity of the horse.
2. Never just pull against the horse, it is much stronger than you are! Use one of the two methods described to achieve a much more effective method of control.
3. Whenever you are riding across country, you must observe the Country Lore and respect the property of others.
4. Always be polite and courteous to other people when you are riding.
5. Practise opening and closing gates as this will reduce the need for you to dismount and remount during a ride.
6. Make sure that you have third party legal liability insurance cover before you ride on the road.
7. Remember that horses must comply with the Highway Code.

INDEX

Page numbers in *italic* refer to the illustrations